Dedicated to Destiny

A Pursuit of Personal Growth, Prosperity & Purpose

Dedicated
to Destiny

A Pursuit of Personal Growth, Prosperity & Purpose

Angel Carlton

CHANGE
MAKERS
BOOKS

Winchester, UK
Washington, USA

First published by Changemakers Books, 2019
Changemakers Books is an imprint of John Hunt Publishing Ltd., No. 3 East Street,
Alresford, Hampshire SO24 9EE, UK
office1@jhpbooks.net
www.johnhuntpublishing.com
www.changemakers-books.com

For distributor details and how to order please visit the 'Ordering' section on our website.

Text copyright: Angel Carlton 2018

ISBN: 978 1 78535 237 9
978 1 78535 238 6 (ebook)
Library of Congress Control Number: 2018943953

A CIP catalogue record for this book is available from the British Library.

Design: Stuart Davies

Printed and bound by CPI Group (UK) Ltd, Croydon, CR0 4YY, UK

We operate a distinctive and ethical publishing philosophy in
all areas of our business, from our global network of authors to
production and worldwide distribution.

Contents

Introduction: My Story of Transformation

Times are changing, and anyone who has a pulse, whether they watch the news or not, will take notice of this undeniable change happening in everyone's life. The world has gotten smaller thanks to the internet, and now we can observe what is happening on the other side of the planet and feel every bit of the intense energy encompassing the globe. For some people it feels like a flipping, rapidly shifting, upside-down and all-around rollercoaster ride. Others may simply brush it off, ignore its tipsy-turns impact, and just go on with their daily life completely unaffected by the collective pain of the human species. It's like there is a new wave of reality under wraps and the only way to conquer it is to somehow blend in with it. The question of the century being asked by millions of people is not so much why—"Why is this happening?"—but how—"How do we survive and get our lives back to a steady and balanced pace?"

One thing I have noticed along the path of my personal evolution is that when life is in alignment with our destiny, there is a feeling of harmony, a natural flow, and there seems to be a subtle order in which things begin to fall into place. On the other hand, I have experienced times when life seems to get off track, feeling like the train suddenly jumps off the rails. The next thing you know is you're flying through the air, not knowing where you will land or how hard the landing may be. This type of unexpected shift in life can be either terrifying or extremely invigorating. Perspective is everything. So many times, we will sit outside of the ride or walk impatiently through that zigzag line for a lifetime, avoiding the thrill of the rollercoaster altogether.

What many don't realize is that it's those ups and downs, twists and turns, and bumpy rides in life that drive us toward our destiny. This is where we discover our purpose, our chosen life path we set forth to unveil. Life is constantly presenting us with opportunities to take either the road that is harmonically aligned with the highest vision we have of ourselves, or the path to simply avoid that evolution altogether. Each unanticipated phase in life is merely a catalyst for change, and these events, as uncomfortable as they may seem, trigger an awakening, an exhilarated exuberance toward living a more fulfilled life. The key is to enjoy the ride, and the only way to enjoy the ride is to become aware of the natural order, the phases, in which life occurs. Once these phases are understood and mastered, we can then effortlessly embark on our sought-after destined path.

By first understanding that change is inevitable, we gain a foundational expectation we can now learn to manage. Only then can we begin believing that one has the power to create a more desirable outcome. This awareness alone can provide enough guidance to break through the barriers that prevent us from navigating the seemingly chaotic times. For so many people, change is happening in one way or another: our relationships are transforming, our sense of security is dwindling, our privacy is diminishing, our government is shifting, and even the weather patterns indicate a planet undergoing turbulent transformation. If you take the time to notice, this shift is happening not just on a personal level, but a global one. Watch the news and see what's happening around our planet; it can be perceived as utter chaos or, from a healthier perspective, a natural process in which change must occur. We can sit back and watch the world "fall apart" or we can do something about it.

Consider this book your call to action and the how-to manual for creating positive change in the world, beginning with yourself. The famous Gandhi saying reminds us to "Be the change you wish to see in the world." We must first align ourselves internally—emotionally, mentally, psychologically, and spiritually with our higher purpose in order for this energy to transfer outwardly to the rest of humanity. If the title of this book piqued your interest, then like me, you have a desire to enhance human lives, starting with improving yours. It's time to intentionally take a leadership role in your own life so you may demonstrate for others another way to exist. It is time to be proactive and not reactive to the ever-changing ways of the world. The time is now for you to take a firm grip on your destiny and stop being bullied by circumstance. Positive change begins with us and it begins within.

In my experience as a corporate leadership trainer, I have observed that all one really needs is perspective and permission: a healthier perspective on life (work, family, etc.) and permission to change. People have been told what they are not allowed to do far more often than being told they *can* do something. Sometimes all people need to hear is "I believe in you" or "You got this" to remind them of their capability. The only way I have found to accomplish this is to simply live it and demonstrate for others another way. Perhaps my perspective will provide you permission to accomplish the changes you seek in your life. Remember, we cannot change other people, but we can influence them to change. Lead your life and others will emulate you.

These changing times can feel like you're in the midst of a hurricane. For many, there is a storm brewing within, with rapidly changing skies on the horizon. Some will take shelter and hide until it passes. Others will fold into the eye of the storm and become a part of the whirlwind. And then there are the storm chasers, the ones who wish to face the cyclone head-on, see it for what it is, and use its powerful force to transform themselves to their next greatest version. It's the only way to truly weather this storm and come out alive, and not just to survive but to thrive as a result of it. That's the easy part. The challenge has been for me not to repeat the same patterns of behavior that originated the storm to begin with. I'll get into greater detail on how we manifest our realities later in this book.

For decades, I have been researching the amazing discoveries of the human spirit and observing the psychology of human behaviors. One consistent fact my studies have revealed is that the collective human species keeps growing and continues to evolve at a rapid pace. Economists recognize this truth as well. In fact, the fastest-growing demographic quickly emerging on our planet is cleverly named the "Cultural Creatives." According to the LOHAS (Lifestyles of Health and Sustainability) demographic studies, Cultural Creatives are identified by their values, beliefs, and lifestyles rather than their purchase of particular products. This tells us that our society is beginning to move from a superficial, materialistic mindset to one that is more humanistic, spiritually meaningful, and compassionate. In a 1999 baseline survey, Cultural Creatives were 26% of American adults. Now Cultural Creatives have grown to nearly 40%!

What does that tell us about where we are heading as a society? Humans are slowly but surely becoming more values-based; that is, heavily driven by solid belief systems. For example, 90.9% of the Cultural Creatives surveyed agree that people need to work for the good of the planet, for it is our only home. To this, I say, "Way to go, humans!" This belief alone is what is driving (no pun intended) the popularity of the Prius and other economically and environmentally friendly vehicles. Whether you currently fall into this demographic or not, we as a society need to create awareness for this impressive group of influencers. We must first establish a firm belief system, then create solid boundaries that inspire ethical choices that lead to a change that is for the good of all. And again, this responsibility begins with you.

People are awakening to another way of existence, one that is connected to not only their highest version of themselves but also a deeper association with the collective human race. The steps outlined in this book will introduce a guide to tie a firm knot with your true self. And once that ribbon is tightened, life will begin to gradually loop together a beautiful bow that attaches you to all of life. The wisdom shared in this book will also provide you with a process to recognize the barriers and clear the clutter that so often prevents us from greatness. Finally, you'll be pointed in the direction of a dedicated destiny that supports your highest purpose, for the good of all, making life the utmost fulfilling experience possible.

Once that clear self-vision has been identified, you have set your firm beliefs in motion, and you begin changing behaviors that align with the new version of yourself, then it's time to pay close attention to the messages that show up. I am a believer that there are no accidents, no such thing as coincidences, that we truly do create every outcome in our lives. My studies, as well as my personal experiences, have proven time and time again that we are the designers of our lives and that serendipity grows from the seed of our imagination. Once we allow our creative beast to go wild and we quiet the scattered mind that tames our passion, we begin to focus the lens, seeing only the stuff that makes our hearts pound and our souls sing. Magic happens when this occurs. That high vibrational energy of your personal passion attracts high vibrational results. Suddenly, the right people will begin popping into your life at the perfect moment, delivering the perfect message. And like a heaven-sent Twitter feed, you'll receive a download of up-to-the-moment messages that will guide you to the finish line.

However, as the saying goes, life is a journey and not a destination, so there will be ongoing obstacles, roadblocks to avoid, and barriers to break down. This book will shine the light on many of them. It is time to embrace the storm, as wildly uncomfortable as it is, knowing it bears gifts of tremendous opportunity for growth. Trust that the Universe has your back and know all changes that occur are purposeful and for your highest good. In time, you will begin to proceed seamlessly without fear and soon discover this destiny-driven space is the most effortless place to reside. Once you prepare yourself for the responsibilities that stem from learning to weather life's storms, assignments will appear. You'll be provided with opportunities like showing others the way by telling your story of transformation, sharing your wisdom, and providing a safe haven, a storm shelter, until the dark clouds pass through the light of their personal evolution.

The reason for sharing all I have learned is due to numerous encounters with devastating cyclones of my own. I understand this process all too well and have seen the power of the Six Stages of Transformation. Those dark clouds rolled in quickly and, without warning, ripped up my cushy lifestyle like a violent tornado. Somehow, I found a way to pick myself up from the ruins. What I am sharing with you in this book is what worked for me to get me back on my path toward my destiny. If David Letterman had a list of the Top 10 Human Stressors, I went through just about all of them all at once. In a matter of a few short months I lost virtually everything, including my home, went through a major financial crisis, a marital separation, relocated out of state, started a new career, and all while trying to maintain my dignity long enough to support my teenage son who was also dealing with the emotional impact of all this change. The turbulence continued as I started a new job, dealt with the loss of both my stepdad and my mother, while traveling 80% of my life, never having a moment to catch up and stabilize.

The truth is, I can look back and say I created much of my own chaos!

If I am to be honest with myself, for many years I resided in a place I call "deniable misery," thinking I was happy but knowing deep down inside there had to be more. Although I had it all on the surface—the big house, family, nice cars, great friends, and my so-called spirituality—I still felt completely unfulfilled. Sure, I went through the motions of daily activities, wearing my happy face. Many times, I was confused by these feelings. My mind and my heart were conflicted. I had things many girls only dream of. I was living the dream in a big beautiful brick home on a golf course, driving a brand-new Lexus, and had just given birth to a beautiful baby boy that I was fortunate enough to stay home with every day. I was married to a great guy with a great sense of humor who worked hard to provide for us every day. "Why isn't this enough?" I would ask myself on a daily basis. In my mind, I knew this was a great life, but my heart had this calling I just could not stop from reappearing and it just kept getting louder and louder. Although I had a wonderful life from the physical, material aspect, these things were not fulfilling. This calling was strong, and something inside me was scratching at me every day reminding me that I have a special mission beyond what the eye can see. "What could be more important or special than raising a child?" I thought.

These feelings persisted. I know I might sound like a spoiled rotten brat, but I kept feeling like there was MORE to life and I wasn't referring to the material stuff. And so my search began. I became a seeker for answers and a searcher for greater wisdom. I spent years thinking, "Maybe this next project will bring me that fulfillment, to get me to that next level of success I so well deserve! That will surely satisfy me." Well, although these creative projects kept me busy they also distracted me from the truth, and the more distracted I got, the more denial played a starring role in my life. If I had only been able to understand what was happening at that time, perhaps I could have saved my marriage instead of destroying it. If I had been aware of my spirit calling me to my destiny instead of blaming everything in my life for my unhappiness, maybe I could have weathered the storm. Little did I know, some of my behaviors were self-destructive and contributed to the destruction of the ones I deeply loved. But I didn't know, not until it was too late.

As if it were a current pulling me down a river, I continued down this unavoidable path toward my destiny, facing many obstacles in the pursuit of my grand purpose. As much as the passion grew, I knew there was something preventing me from attaining that vision. I became a pro at seemingly being "pulled together" on the outside, while on the inside I felt lost, lacked direction, and my internal navigation system was seemingly recalibrating. I knew it was a matter of time until others would see that it was all just a facade, and my smile was merely a mask that soon would be revealed. I found that sooner or later, truth finds you. There just comes a time in life when you find the courage to look in the mirror, only to see a different reflection of yourself. As if you're seeing yourself for the first time, disbelief seeps in as you try to find some resemblance of happiness, the person you dreamed you'd be when you were younger. Where did she go? Who is this person and who has she become? It was as if I were looking at a stranger, a person I had seen every day of my life, but didn't recognize. It was the first time I literally held up the mirror to myself and, in this exact moment of awareness, a transformational turning point would prevail. Change was evident, leaving me with no choice other than to see the truth as it is and to finally stop living the lie I had been. As Buddha once said, "Three things cannot be long hidden: the sun, the moon, and the truth."

My unmanageable turmoil soon became my turning point. I blamed my marriage for being the cause of my feeling unfulfilled when in reality it was simply my spirit trying to grasp my attention and that of my husband. If I had been more aware, I would have known we were supposed to travel the destined path together. But I didn't and so our marriage soon began to shift and our family dynamic was forever changed.

While my situation was wildly uncomfortable, the new environment had an undercurrent of peacefulness as catastrophic life-change was underway. The warmth of my parents' "summer home" provided my son and me with a safe space to heal our emotional wounds and rejuvenate our spirits. Little did I know at the time, the next couple of years were going to be the most amazing growth period of my entire life and I have to believe the same applied to my son as well. And so the healing process began. For weeks, it seemed, I would have spontaneous outbreaks of crying, sometimes sobbing so strongly I couldn't catch my breath, many times lying in bed cuddled up in a fetal position, scared and uncertain of what the future would hold. My spirit would occasionally rise above, look down at its own body, and observe the scene. I felt a gentle nudge, a reminder that this was part of the releasing phase, that it was my soul cleansing itself as if it were being showered after being dragged through the mud.

As I rose above and observed my own victim-like behavior, I began to develop a new and quite refreshing self-awareness. This interesting excavation of what felt like a lifetime of bottled-up energy was not coming from a place of sadness or self-pity, but more of a miraculous healing of this emotional pain I never even knew existed. Something deep inside me had been shaken up. It seems the drastic change had given me a new perspective and I was able to see how very stressful my life had become. Not just during the previous year but over the past several years. I had been telling myself a story of untruths, wearing a mask of happiness, fooling everyone and, truthfully, "white-knuckling" through life. I was so busy creating the perfect life to feel accepted by everyone else, I had forgotten about the mission of my soul. I had been going against the current of my own purpose and fighting the flow of life.

Those tears were certainly cleansing tears. My soul was quietly rejoicing. My spirit was slowly coming out of hiding, and like seeing a glimpse of a rainbow through a vigorous waterfall, I was beginning to see the beauty in my life again. What is really strange is that I had to lose everything—I mean *everything*—for me to realize that I had not been living authentically, that I had just been affected by life's circumstances. I was the victim being bullied by my own mind, thoughts, and beliefs. This is when I made the decision to not stay in this place and to begin the rebuilding process. It was a period of rebounding from the fall. I have heard this saying: "If you're going to fail...fail fast." And I say, "If you've fallen, rebound ferociously and bounce back enthusiastically." Literally, get up as quickly as possible, brush off your knees and shake it off. I now had the incredible opportunity of a lifetime to reinvent myself and have one more shot at fulfilling my purpose. So, in my mid-forties, I began again.

Clarity slowly began to shine through the clouds of doubt and worry. In order to break free from chaos, sometimes you have to take drastic measures and steamroll through it all, even if the only thing waiting to greet you on the other side is the unknown. It's the ultimate test of faith and trust. It's interesting, the immediate connection to Spirit, God, or Source we suddenly have when the blindfold is on and we are unable to see where we're going. Oh, how I had missed my beautiful relationship, the closeness of my silent spiritual friend of hope, my invisible guide and guardian, the almighty, always-present comrade and my biggest fan. "We have reunited," I thought to myself, "and it feels so good." (The oldie but goodie Peaches & Herb song is suddenly playing in my head.)

Then one magical day comes when you realize you have arrived at the other side of the confusion. This surreal feeling is indescribable. I guess that is to be expected when one abruptly departs one life for another. It's a strange and bizarre state of consciousness, in which everything seems part of a crazy dream. Apprehensive about my next steps, I cautiously remained aware of the fear of falling out of this "flow" so as not to find myself back where I came from. So, I joyously sat in silence, listening for the next message, the next small step to take me through this unknown place. A friend told me, "You don't have to see the whole staircase, just the first step." These words rang true as I remained engaged in the present moment where I felt safe from that harmful, destructive poison called fear.

Our journeys are what we make of them, and from our choices

we either evolve or we divert. A rather peculiar opportunity presented itself while I sat in the most uncertain phase of my life. This is when I realized it was not a time to sit in my comfort zone waiting for things to change. This was a time to stretch myself beyond my wildest imagination, to take the challenges that showed up, and to be reminded of the inner power I've always had. As I entered the reinventing stage of transformation and my energy was generating a positive vibration again, a friend called to offer me an amazing job! This was the perfect opportunity to practice my "new self" and, at the same time, one of the greatest life challenges I've had. This new position is what got my career back on track and I am forever grateful for that friend who believed in me even though she knew what I had been going through.

This was an easy choice to make since it was the only opportunity showing up at this time. How ironic, I thought, the project that showed up after I was coming out of the lowest part of my life was to teach others how to become a better leader. I have done public speaking in the past and certainly have a passion for making a difference in people's lives, but I honestly questioned my own capability. The truth is, I was in no position to let fear get the best of me this time! This was my only option and I knew I couldn't fail. I needed something this drastic, this challenging, for me to break the lifetime cycle of self-sabotaging doubt.

Through this rewarding work, I continue to learn so much about myself, my gifts, my strengths, my courage, my perseverance, and my determination. I have learned that this transformational period of my life has only prepared me for something greater, for accomplishments I have yet to experience and abilities I have yet to know…for my destiny. A purpose that is not just to better my own life, but the ringing in my ear that calls upon me to be proactive in the societal shift and reach out to the distressed, collective human spirit. I know I am here to make a difference, big or small, and create positive change on this planet by sharing my story and the process that got me here.

It's important for us to do our best while we are here in this life, to make it a better place than when we arrived so that future generations can thrive. There are so many humans suffering as I have. It would be selfish to sit on the sidelines and watch the struggles of humanity, knowing what I have learned. The light at the end of the dark tunnel comes with a responsibility to show others the way out of darkness. Unannounced perseverance shows up when we need it and proves to us that our spirit is stronger than our minds can ever be. That when we focus on our growth, this means our spirit is at work and following through on its purpose. And we all come here, to this planet, with a purposeful mission. This is the reason changes happen and choices are made, for us to take one path or another. Although I have had many paths to choose from, all my opportunities and experiences have led me to the same place, reminding me to stay true to myself. Through all the choices I have made, my entire life story leads to one truth, one self-discovery, one realization: I am dedicated to my destiny.

The self-dedications or strategies outlined in this book stem from my personal growth experiences and an observation of my personal evolution into the next phase of my life journey. I began to outline all of the things that have worked for me to get me out of a lonely place of discontent to a fulfilling, purposeful, abundant life. This place is where dreams are manifested and miracles are a daily occurrence. As I reflected back on this tremendous personal evolution, I began to realize that life is but a cycle, and after much pondering, I have been able to break the process of change into **Six Stages of Transformation**: Realize, Release, Rebound, Reinvent, Resurrect, and Respond.

It is through these six phases that I have experienced profound changes in my personal self. I noticed that as I made a conscious choice to change certain behaviors, discipline myself, and gain balance, I began to see a substantial shift in the direction of my life. Consider this book a manual for a more prosperous life. I am living proof that when someone dedicates their life to their higher purpose, life begins to fall into place seamlessly, effortlessly, and harmonically. If you feel your destiny is just on the horizon, and you are feeling called to a higher purpose, then use this book as your guide. Practice the exercises, put into practice what I have, and continue to utilize this guidebook toward creating your next highest version of who you are. The outcome will astound you as you observe the evolution of your destined self.

To practice self-discipline is to become the disciple of your own destiny. What that essentially means is to become a leader and, at the same time, a follower, a student and observer of your life experience. When you engage with your higher self, your soul guide, internal life teacher, and all-knowing philosopher, your world becomes meaningful. Life suddenly feels exceptionally fulfilling as you now see the alignment of all your choices, and how every moment of your human existence has led you to this very word you are reading on this page.

The dedications outlined in this book, when practiced and applied, will move you to self-discover your destined self. At the end of every chapter you will find a self-discovery section, offering ways to remind you of your true path, accelerate your spiritual evolution, and create harmony and balance in your life. I encourage you to have a dedicated journal as you engage in the thought-provoking, soul-searching exercises. I invite you to make this book a personal development experience, a mini-workshop, for yourself or with your partner, friends, or a study group. It is essential to understand where you are, where you've been, and where you're heading, so let's begin first by breaking down the Six Stages of the Transformation Cycle.

Overview of the Six Stages of Transformation

CHAPTER / STAGE	REALIZE	RELEASE	REBOUND	REINVENT	RESURRECT	RESPOND
1 AWARENESS FREES/ACCEPTANCE HEALS (RESONATE)	X					
2 VISUALIZE THE PRIZE (REMEMBER)	X					
3 LIVE IN TRUTH (RESUSCITATE)	X					
4 ALIGN YOUR ALLIES (RELIEVE)		X				
5 OPEN DOOR SYNDROME (RE-EVALUATE)		X				
6 SECRETS, FEARS & TEARS (REVEAL)		X				
7 REVIVE YOUR SPIRIT (RECUPERATE, REJUVENATE & REBALANCE)			X			
8 LIVE REGRET-FREE (REPROGRAM)				X		
9 CREATE A NEW STORY (REDEFINE)				X		
10 BECOME YOUR OBSERVER (REACQUAINT)				X		
11 MANAGE YOUR ENERGY (REMAIN)					X	
12 COMMIT WITH PURPOSE (RESPECT)					X	
13 DEDICATE TO DESTINY (RESOLVE)					X	
14 BUILD THE BRIDGE (REACT)						X

The beauty in breaking down our transformational process is that, as I mentioned in the introduction, you can see where you've been, where you are, and where you're heading. Keep in mind that like everything in life, this is a cycle and is in constant motion. This is the same process every time a life change is experienced. You may be in the Reinventing phase one week and Realize phase the next. You may feel the oneness of the Resurrect stage one day, then swoop into Releasing stage. You are constantly experiencing at least one or all of these phases at any given time throughout your life and on multiple levels. Learning to manage the process is key. Think of it as a spiral staircase. Each step is another stage of transformation. Every step you take gets you closer to the next level of understanding. Enlightened perspectives and unexpected opportunities greet you at each level.

This is the personal approach to transformation, but how can knowing this information impact the world? The world has become a messy place, filled with violence, anger, and destruction. Many people ask me, "What can we do to change this? How will personal transformation create positive change in the world?"

Much like climbing up a spiral staircase, the first step is that life-changing event that occurs, the wake-up call that propels you upward, that earth-shattering epiphany that forces you to **realize** something needs to change. The winding, narrow steps may be somewhat intimidating and confusing at first. Your curiosity gets the best of you as you see this staircase leading to some unknown place, somewhere you've never been. You can see the shimmering of a light at the top that is so intriguing you feel an urge to investigate this spiritual pull. So you grab the railing, pull yourself up slowly, and cautiously take your first step. Your very first step on this mystical spiral already makes you feel like life will never be the same.

As you climb and wind yourself around the staircase, changing your perspective a bit, you finally see what is happening. You approach the second turn, take a quick glance at the steps below, and suddenly become aware of the lesson you learned from your first step, whether it be tragic or joyous. You begin to see the strain you have endured over the years, the emotional baggage from your past, and the unnecessary weight you've been carrying with you. Finally, the point has come to **release** it as you realize this heavy load won't be beneficial to you as you climb the staircase. Furthermore, you've become tired of trekking with this weight and finally acknowledge that these things haven't really helped you in any way and it's time to leave them behind.

As you climb the stairway, you feel a sense of lightness; perhaps it feels empty, like an unfamiliar void, like something is missing from your life. And truthfully, there is something missing...you! You'll soon begin to see the need to fill this awkward space; part of you even wants to go back down the stairs to grab the baggage you left behind, thinking you may need it. After all it's familiar, it's what you know, unlike the twisting unfamiliar stairwell you're climbing. You look back and take one last look at what you've released and that comfy old blanket of beliefs you've taken with you everywhere you've gone—*until now*, that is. You take a moment to catch your breath, recover, and **rebound** from the climb. You may shed a tear or two, feel sad at the loss, and long for the past, but you soon begin to feel a different feeling of security and support now and it is within you. This feeling is called faith. This is where the real courage is required. Do you step back down to where you've been? Or do you proceed up the stairs, taking another step toward the direction of your destiny? Of course you proceed, because you are dedicated to fulfilling your destiny, this burning desire and calling that screams for your attention. This is when you fill that space with the components of who you have always wanted to be. The person who is no longer influenced by others, but by the guidance of your own soul.

The most extreme version of your "best you" is on the horizon. You begin to envision this ultimate being of self, and in that process you create yourself anew. With every step, you begin to **reinvent** a higher, more powerful version of who you are. And you become empowered, stepping more confidently toward this vision of grandeur.

Before you know it, you see the top of the staircase. The bright, welcoming light shining through the glass ceiling is so bright you may be tempted to turn and go back to the place where you could see. The blinding light of the unknown is scary, but it doesn't stop you. Why? Because you have come too far to turn back now. You are past the point of no return and your destiny is shining at you, welcoming you with open arms. It's yours for the taking! So you begin to pick up the pace, even taking two steps at a time, as you anxiously bolt toward the top of the staircase. And just before reaching the top, you pause. You look back at how far you have come, where the journey of life began. And you see all the perfection in each experience, every relationship that you labeled good, bad, or otherwise. You now see that every turning point, every step along the way, was so purposeful for you to be exactly where you are now. The feeling is an overwhelming sense of peace followed by an outbreak of gratitude and appreciation for the road you chose to travel. A magical journey indeed, like no other. And so you rise above the fears, the worries, and the doubts that have controlled you and you **resurrect** toward your vision.

But wait! There is movement down below. You peek over the railing and look down the winding staircase. You see a hand on the railing; it's someone struggling to take their first step. They look weary and doubtful. Their baggage is weighing them down and they stop as if they are ready to give up and go back. Your destined self now has a responsibility, a new calling…to simply **respond**. And so, without hesitation, you meet the person where they are on the staircase, extend your reach, take their hand, comfort them, and help them take a step onto the next phase of life. Your story gives hope, inspires and encourages them to keep going. They are grateful.

It's time to put the kindness back into humankind and help one another, hold up the mirror and show others their personal power and encourage them to do the same. It's time to pay forward your reward. You've been up and down the staircase of life; you have experienced the Six Stages of Transformation and have evolved toward your destined self. Use your power wisely and help those who are dedicated to destiny to fulfill theirs too. A difference-maker or light-worker can always recognize the light in others. It is our responsibility to spark that light at times when theirs has dimmed.

In summary, this cycle of personal growth is a pattern in which we are continuously learning about ourselves. Every life choice, experience or event takes us into the next phase of development. At each phase of this cycle we move into a higher level of self-awareness. Let's recap these stages so that the brain will have one more opportunity to soak it all in.

Stage 1—REALIZE. Realize is the "aha" moment, a new realization about yourself and your relationship to life; a new and improved vision of who you are and what you expect out of life begins to develop; becoming self-aware of the change happening and your own personal evolution that is about to take place.

Stage 2—RELEASE. Release stage is when you begin releasing the external components of your life that no longer serve you, leaving behind the "emotional baggage" mostly caused by former relationships, disappointments, or upsets. Letting go of the unhealthy habits, patterns of thinking, and beliefs creates space for you to reinvent yourself.

Stage 3—REBOUND. Rebound is the phase in which you nurture your mind, body, and spirit by allowing time to process any recent life changes so that you can ease into the integration of the next level of transformation.

Stage 4—REINVENT. Reinvent is another self-focused phase where you are making new choices that are in alignment with the self-realized vision in the first phase, Realize. It is the empty space that begs to be filled with new choices, behaviors, and habits that are purposeful and productive.

Stage 5—RESURRECT. Resurrect is when you begin to rise above the obstacles that have held you back in the past; you begin to flow with life and listen to your inner voice for guidance rather than depend on past beliefs. You begin to see life differently and feel a calling to "pay forward" your learned lessons and share your newfound wisdom with others. Your desire to make a difference in the world begins to grow as you find ways to enlighten others with your insights. You are living in a higher state of awareness and enlightenment.

Stage 6—RESPOND. Respond is the stage when you begin asking, "What can I do? How can I contribute to making a positive impact in my life and ultimately in the world?" For starters, set a firm intention to become a better leader, a stronger communicator, and an exemplary role model for others, especially our younger generations.

If there is one thing we know from living life, it is that change will happen. Embrace life as an ongoing process of transformation and retain a healthy curiosity about each outcome. These stages are simply a way for personal development to become more sustainable in an ever-changing world. It is your prescription for a healthy, fulfilled, and dedicated life.

Part 1

Realize

The First Stage of Transformation

Chapter 1

Awareness Frees & Acceptance Heals (Resonate)

Whenever we experience any sort of change in our lives, it is either shocking, surprising, or stops us in our tracks. Now life offers us basically three choices. First, to accept what is happening; second, to slip into denial or avoid it altogether; and third, to keep white-knuckling through life pretending like we have control when we really don't. This is the time to stop and ask yourself which one of those resonates as the truth for you. If you choose to avoid the situation and keep sweeping it under the rug, don't be surprised if it shows up again in another unexpected, disappointing experience. Once you create the awareness around the fact that these events happen for your good, you will see that they are intentionally moving you from where you are in your life to where you were destined to be.

Many people become complacent with being unhappy and miserable. It's true! I was there myself. It was just easier to stay in a situation where I knew I wasn't growing, just because moving on would rock the boat too much. And rocking the boat creates waves. Waves eventually impact others. This is why it is vitally important to become consciously aware of the changes in your life, and act accordingly so that it will have a positive impact, not only on your life, but also on the lives of everyone who will feel the effects of the ripple. Change, when approached delicately and deliberately, is one of our greatest teachers.

Perhaps the change you are going through at this particular time is a loss, either a job lost, a loved one's passing, a relationship ending, or just feeling lost. These are perfect opportunities for you to shift your life and move it into that dream life you have always known exists deep down inside your soul. Perhaps you feel you took a wrong turn or made a poor choice or two, and that's what got you to feeling like there is more to life than what you're experiencing. Regardless of what the change is, it is time to first accept that it is happening for a good reason. Second, know that you have total control of the outcome.

Any change in life that occurs, whether by choice or by chance, requires our 360-degree awareness in order to move through it with ease and grace. Otherwise, we will fight it, fear it, and forget it. You will see that when you do this, it will appear down the road and it won't be any easier to deal with then. In fact, it may appear as anger, stress, or even violence when those emotions of change are kept inside and not properly dealt with. Embrace the process to navigate change so that you come out shining on the other side. Shining like the brightest star in the sky. Shining that light on the sea of darkness like a lighthouse in the night. You will light up the lives of others when you ignite change with intention, awareness, and acceptance.

It is time to acknowledge what is happening in your life and trust that it is happening for the betterment of yourself. Trust that whatever it is you are going through has a message, a life lesson and purpose. But you cannot identify the beauty of change until you face it and see it for what it is. You will need to take off the blinders in order to see the gift the life-altering event has to deliver. There is some inner work involved. Are you willing to put in some effort so that you can fulfill your destiny? Are you willing to remove the blindfold of your past and face some unhappy times in order to create space for the ultimate happiness? Are you willing to face your past in order to create your future? This takes courage. It takes perseverance. It requires support, all of which you possess. It is time to face your greatest fears and unrevealed feelings of the past. The time is now to bring them into the light and welcome them into your life. Once you do this, they dissolve forever. After all, fear just wants to be seen. I invite you to do this worthwhile work. I know the benefits. If I can do it, so can you. I believe in you. I truly do.

Once you know how to deal with change in a positive and productive way, you then become the pillar on which to help others deal with change. I am giving you permission to boldly step into that role and know you have the capacity to inspire positive change in your circle of influence. But it has to start with you. It begins with a devoted self-awareness and a humble approach toward acceptance. It has to start by clearing the emotional baggage; those barriers and blocks that have kept your light dim over the years. This process will help you heal those aspects of your life so that you may begin again, a new life that inspires love, laughter, and leadership. Let us begin by taking a few minutes to engage with ourselves in some self-discovery time.

Self-Discovery:

- In one short sentence, identify the change you are experiencing.
- Describe the feelings you have when you think of this change.
- Face those feelings and say these words: "I see you (state the feeling), I honor your power, and thank you for showing me another aspect of myself."
- How would it feel to have yourself be your very best friend, the one you can count on for everything?

Chapter 2

Visualize the Prize (Remember)

Morning approaches and you begin to awake from a long night's rest. Slowly your mind begins to depart from your sleep state, toggling back and forth between your dream and reality. Your alarm is going off, your eyes open, your mind re-engages in the moment, and within an instant you shift from the illusory state and are suddenly jolted back into the "reality" of what has become your present life. This reality is the actuality of the life you have created thus far...good, bad, happy, or sad, this is your world that you exist in every day when you wake up. Just another opportunity for you to make the change you so desire, personally, professionally, spiritually, emotionally, or physically.

Perhaps the day has arrived when that one glorious event occurs that changes everything, be it an epiphany, a tragedy, or a mere thought. I am referring to those rare experiences that cause you to pause and completely, sometimes suddenly, change your perspective on life and the purpose of your existence. This is the moment when all the thoughts you currently held about yourself, even lifelong beliefs up until that point, are now in question. It's where everything you thought you knew suddenly becomes blurred by an unknown, unidentified, and unexpected clarity. An inexpressible feeling of expansion fills your being, bringing a renewed sense of self-awareness, a rise in self-esteem, and a calling for self-evaluation.

It's not long after this point that you begin to ask questions from this secondary perspective. Questions like "Who am I?", "Why am I here?", "Is this all there is?", or "What is the purpose of my life?" It is in these deep and transformational questions that things begin to shift. This is a turning point, this is the fork in the road, this is what is referred to as a spiritual awakening, a remembrance of who you truly are; when your spirit hops into the driver's seat, takes the wheel and begins driving you toward your destiny. Or you can look at it as if your mind has finally surrendered and quieted itself long enough for you to actually feel the essence of your soul. Finally, you hear the calling of your own spirit that has been trying to get your attention for as long as you have been in your human body.

Whatever brought you to this point is irrelevant; what you need to embrace is the fact that this is a turning point and where you go from here is completely up to you. It's time to feel empowered as you begin to embark on a new path in life. The truth is, once you have this awareness, you are past the point of no return. This means that once you recognize this unusual shift in how you perceive life, your spirit has made its appearance, making it extremely difficult to ignore its existence. And so the journey truly begins...the journey to the center of...you.

With the inquiry of self, you are on a mission to find answers to the questions you have been asking. You find yourself reading books you never thought you'd read, attending conferences or study groups with people you never thought you'd associate with, and exploring new opportunities for growth, all to seek more clarity on this awkward state of awareness. Your vision begins with a glimpse through the naked eye; perhaps a reflection in the mirror triggers your spiritual memory. Then as you begin to turn the focus knob to zoom in on the next highest vision, you gaze through your spiritual binoculars to get a closer look. You find yourself closing in on something you're not quite able to identify, like trying to get a glimpse of the wings of a beautiful butterfly fluttering around. All you know is you must continue to identify it, focus on it, and seek more clarity. This seeking and searching becomes a healthy addiction; you feel alive again and now you're beginning to understand there is more to life than what you previously thought. Your spirit has awakened. You realize the beautiful butterfly has transformed from the cocoon and although the freedom of having wings is extraordinary, the light outside is a complete mystery to the emerging insect. The day has come for you to take off the blinders and see yourself as the incredible, amazing gift to the world that you are. It is time for you to discover why you are here and the greater purpose you are here to serve. This is your time...your time to become more intentional about the outcome of your life and dedicate yourself to your destiny.

The journey of your awakened self begins with one big question: Who is the person I am destined to become? You know there's more to you than has been discovered. You feel an opening, a portal, to another side that hasn't quite yet been explored. The follow-up question is: How? How do I unleash the being, the life force within that has waited a lifetime to be freed?

Stephen Covey said it best in his book, 7 *Habits of Highly Effective People*: "Begin with the end in mind." If you don't know where you're heading, you will never get there—it's that simple. So as we embark on this journey, even if you have been on your path for a while, there are two things to understand: first, where you are now, and second, where are you heading. I mean, really look at your life and see what direction you need to point your compass in. Then recognize where you're going and then take your first step in that direction. It will require courage, discipline, and perseverance; however, you can move through the discomfort of your shaken-up life with ease and certainty with the steps I am outlining for you here in this book. I believe in you and it's time you believe in yourself too.

First, let's look at where you've been, then we can determine where you are, and finally you'll have a clear outlook on where you're heading. You may be in a place of mundane routine, a limiting environment for growth, fearful of stepping out and doing something different, even doubting your own ability to do it. You may be experiencing a low energy vibration, where you are always feeling tired, easily exhausted, and your energy is being drained.

This is typically when we notice ourselves in a very unhappy state, an unfulfilled place, a totally unproductive time of life. You might be feeling "stuck in the middle of nowhere," where nothing fulfills you, and yet you feel a calling, a yearning to do and become something greater than you currently are. "Nowhere" can be a lonely place. Suddenly you find yourself there, looking around for some familiarity of who you used to be, but that person is nowhere to be found. Why? Because transformation is underway and most likely you didn't have the end in mind.

The basic definition of the Law of Entropy is: *what is left alone for an extended period of time will resort to its lowest form of energy*. When we allow life, or our untamed minds, to control our direction, we tend to get sidetracked by circumstance and end up separating ourselves from our spirit. When this disconnect occurs, for any amount of time, we become detached from life because our egos end up taking control, convincing us to fulfill temporary desires. Yet, the authentic desires of our spirit, the human soul, are sitting in the back of the bus the ego has been driving, just waiting for the next stop. It's usually not until the bus crashes that "spirit" gets invited to step up and drive.

Many times our choices, behaviors, and actions are the result of being affected *by* life, rather than being the "affecter." Something I want to remind you of is: we as humans are made of three parts, our mind, our body, and our spirit. Think of your spirit as your compass to guide you toward your destiny (because it knows why it's here). Your compass is always there to remind you when you're off track and heading in another direction. The trick is to understand and become consciously aware of when this occurs so that you can tune back into the compass for direction. Your body is your vehicle to transport your spirit on your life journey of evolution, and your mind is to protect you with necessary worldly information and the knowledge gained from your human experience. There are times when the mind, or ego, needs to be the bus driver in this competitive world of ours and that's okay—you just have to be sure you're giving it permission to do so. With keen awareness and practice you can maintain a proper balance between spirit and ego. To find one's destiny one must "synergize" (I'm not sure that's even a word but using it anyway) its three parts. We exercise our bodies to stay in shape, and we sharpen our minds by reading and constantly learning, but when was the last time you paid any attention to your destiny-driven spirit?

You may have been driving blindly without a map, not utilizing your compass to assist you in getting to your destination... UNTIL NOW. These are the two most powerful words in the English language when combined: "UNTIL NOW." Following up any self-sabotaging statement with these two simple words will immediately inspire change, wipe the slate clean, and put into action whatever positive change you wish to create. This will immediately send a message to the Universe letting it know you are no longer being or doing that "old" way and to stay tuned as you begin to create the new and improved version of yourself. Begin now to implement these words in your daily vocabulary and self-talk. Try it for yourself and see how this will shift your energy by immediately releasing that old belief pattern. "Oh I could never do that!" UNTIL NOW! "That's just not me." UNTIL NOW! "I don't have the confidence to become that person." UNTIL NOW! I am sure you're beginning to get the picture and feel the power of "UNTIL NOW."

There is a reason I introduced "UNTIL NOW" in this first part of the book; because it is one habit you can begin to implement at every phase of your spiritual awakening—and the sooner you do, the more quickly your desired outcome will appear. Say it loud and say it often. Let's face it, the current beliefs and stories you've been telling yourself (you know, the ones that keep you small and insignificant) have gotten you to this forsaken place to begin with. It's time to break free and head to that place of certainty, purpose, and complete freedom as your life was designed to be. It's time to enter the euphoric place of knowing exactly who you are, what you want, why you're here, what you're supposed to be doing, where anything is possible and life becomes a limitless adventure every day upon awakening.

To experience an abundant life a person must identify and change their behaviors. A behavior is an action you can see or hear; otherwise it's just an opinion, a judgment, or a belief. In order to change outcomes, you must change your behaviors. For example, if I wanted to change the number that shows up on my scale every morning when I weigh myself, I would have to discover the behavior that needed to change. That outcome will never change unless I change my eating and exercise habits. Changing lifelong habitual patterns is not always easy. It's been my personal experience that change is sometimes difficult, but always worthwhile. The first step in changing behavioral patterns is to identify them, and we will address this momentarily.

Here's how I see it: In order to arrive at your destination (place of your destiny), you must set the navigation system (your mind) and use a compass (your spirit) to guide you in the direction toward that fulfilled and purposeful life you've only imagined...UNTIL NOW. This is why it is gravely important that you take the time right now to envision yourself in your highest form. I invite you to pause for a moment, engage your spirit, and recall a snapshot of yourself before society took a toll on your soul. Remember your destined self, the dedicated one who showed up on this planet with a purpose. You may have to revisit your childhood to find this person as you begin to recognize the choices you made that took you off this path. Perhaps you can even identify behaviors that have gotten you to this stagnant place.

This inner work can sometimes be emotionally disturbing, as our egos never want to admit mistakes. Let me remind you, there are no mistakes, mishaps or failures in life. Everything that has occurred has happened to get you to this place, where you are on this very day right now. No matter what choices you have made, what path you would have taken, your experiences are part of your own evolution. It's time to own your own leadership, hold up the mirror, and see yourself in a new reflection. I am here to do two things: provide perspective and give permission. Because I have resurrected through my own transformation, and continue to intentionally evolve with every changing circumstance in my life, I am able to provide another perspective for you and your life while granting you permission to change whatever it is that no longer serves you. You hold the power. I truly believe in you. I believe in the power of the human spirit.

As you move into the self-discovery section of this chapter, I invite you to envision yourself living out your full potential, and don't hold back. It's time to remember your true self, the person you intended to be when your spirit took its physical human form. Open your mind, expand your heart, and let the power of your imagination run wild to see what thoughts, visions, and inspirations show up during this process. Let's begin with discovering your vision, the "end in mind" as it relates to your purpose, and begin the process that will take you to your destiny. Visualize the prize, and the prize is you living in your highest version of yourself.

Remember to take notes immediately after your visualization process and jot down any self-discoveries. I highly recommend a personal journal or dedicated notepad. Record anything that shows up, especially the vision that makes you smile. Be also aware of any fears or patterns of thinking, emotional triggers, thoughts of people, places, or memories, as these are all crucial in discovering the blocks that prevent you from being your highest version of yourself. Also, pay attention to the thoughts that may be "gateways" to your destiny, as this could be spirit communicating with you in that open space you created by quieting your mind. So let's get you on your way. Take some time to marinate yourself in self-discovery.

Self-Discovery:

- Clear your mind for a moment and just breathe. Then, imagine yourself living out your full potential, your greatest self-vision. What is the first thing that comes to mind?
- Continue to visualize that image in a relaxed state of mind and journal the answers to these questions:

  A. What do you look like? (Well-groomed, confident, well-dressed, physically fit, etc.)
  B. Describe your emotional state.
  C. How does your highest version walk into a crowded room? (Do you "own it" or quietly enter with little attention? What is your posture like?)
  D. Who is in the room? (Are there people in your life currently, from the past, or people you don't know?)
  E. What is the response of others as you enter the room? (Do they stop their conversations, look up to see you, smile at you, or do they go about their business?)
  F. How do you greet them? (Do you proactively approach people to shake hands, look them in the eyes and feel genuinely happy to see them?)
  G. How do they greet you? (Enthusiastically, hesitantly, eagerly, etc.)
  H. Are you fully engaged in that moment and genuinely happy to be in the presence of others?
  I. When someone you are speaking to asks you to speak of your wisdom, what is the message you share?

- Write down everything you recall from your vision in a journal.
- In your journal, make a note of which of the six phases you feel you are currently in right now (Realize, Release, Rebound, Reinvent, Resurrect, Respond).
- Create a KNOWING BOARD or binder with visuals of

yourself fully expressed; cut these out from magazines or find images on the internet that best describe your higher self. Revisit these visuals on a regular basis so that they seep into your subconscious mind.

- Think about the three parts of your being (mind, body, spirit).

   A. Is your mind in alignment with your destiny/vision? (If yes, what is the one word to describe that thought? If no, what's preventing you from focusing on your vision?)

   B. Does your body resemble the one in your vision? (If yes, what behaviors do you wish to continue? If no, what's preventing you from obtaining the physical picture of yourself?)

   C. Does your spirit feel like it's on the right track? (If yes, describe the feeling. If no, describe what it will feel like when it is.)

   D. Does your mind reflect a healthy image of yourself? (If yes, describe that image in three words. If no, what thought patterns need to change?)

- On a scale from 1 to 10 (1 = not even close to your highest vision, 10 = living this vision fully), where are you right now? Chart where you feel you are today and revisit the graph to chart your progress daily, weekly, monthly, etc. You can indicate Mind by placing an "M" on your chart, "B" for Body, and "S" for Spirit. You will be able to track your growth and progress as you continue to self-discover and move through each of the six phases of personal transformation, join the dots and see for yourself the positive trend you are creating for yourself. Just commit to doing the work.

Mark the graph with today's date where you feel you are at this moment. Do this for the current state of your mind, body and spirit. Revisit this graph after putting the principles in this book into practice. Gauge your growth every week, month or year.

Mind = *I often see and visualize my highest vision with clarity.*

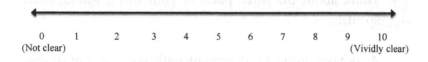

| 0 | 1 | 2 | 3 | 4 | 5 | 6 | 7 | 8 | 9 | 10 |
(Not clear)   (Vividly clear)

Body = *I embrace and embody the highest vision of how I look and represent myself physically.*

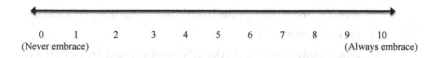

| 0 | 1 | 2 | 3 | 4 | 5 | 6 | 7 | 8 | 9 | 10 |
(Never embrace)   (Always embrace)

Spirit = *I feel aligned with my highest purpose and I feel ultimately fulfilled.*

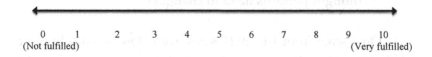

| 0 | 1 | 2 | 3 | 4 | 5 | 6 | 7 | 8 | 9 | 10 |
(Not fulfilled)   (Very fulfilled)

Chapter 3

Live in Truth (Resuscitate)

This chapter is where we literally resuscitate, or bring back to life the "true self." In order to do this, one must align with the truth. This is not an easy task. Truth is certainly an interesting topic. Its real definition is: *that which is true or in accordance with fact or reality.* I invite you to consider another perspective on "truth" in its most raw form. Since we are all living out our own version of reality, it would appear as though we each have our own version of truth. Our personal experiences certainly create what we perceive as truth. What's true to one may not be true to another. My question is, can we then call that "Truth"? I have caught myself tossing truth around like a hot potato when I've said things like, "My truth is this..." or "That's not my truth," as if I have the power to own "truth." I have realized there is a fine line between defining my truth and rationalizing a situation. And in my personal experience, rationalizing has been one of "my (unhealthy) truths" that I have notoriously used to justify my questionable behaviors, thoughts, and feelings. This realization has caused me to use that term lightly, if at all. I find it much more enlightening to speak more from the "inclusionary" truth, as Caroline Myss has described it, "to avoid creating separation between myself and the opposing truth."

There is a difference between truth and perspective. My experiences have built my beliefs, which can be identified as my truth; however, beliefs change, therefore my opinion may change—but truth shouldn't change at all if it is truly true. So I just caution everyone to use this term gently and consider all perspectives so that we are not separating ourselves or making ourselves "better" in any way. No right or wrong here, just creating awareness. Each of us has our own beliefs that make up our truth. So, I see it as a giant puzzle where each person has a piece of truth, their own reality based on their own beliefs. When we put all of these pieces of truth together, we have the big picture, Truth.

This is the point in your personal growth when you have to see not just your truth but *the* Truth; after all, what's been true for you so far may not be serving you best anyway.

Get ready to use your CPR training because it is time to resuscitate the truth. The "inclusive" truth that all can see. Truth in its purest form creates unity, whereas "my truth" can potentially create separation. Look at the violent belief system in the Middle East. There are people there who despise the United States to the point of violence and destruction; this is their sad and disturbing truth. To most, it's unfathomable that people can have such a belief system. The inclusive truth says we are all one, connected in spirit, and when you destroy one of us, you destroy all of us.

Notice when you begin to rationalize the truth, bend it and twist it, to protect your own ego. Acknowledging this is not an easy thing to do, as our egos will fight to be right at any cost. One way to know the difference between the truths your ego is telling you to believe and the Truth is the emotional reaction when you first hear or learn of this truth. I have always said, "Truth is absurd when first heard." Think about it: most truth comes to us as being somewhat shocking, and the first reaction is to reject it. For example, a sudden death takes place in your family. It's an "inclusive" undeniable truth, but we fight it because the mind doesn't want it to be so. It takes an open mind to really let the Truth settle in and find a place to resonate. Another symptom of truth is when you find it difficult to have a conversation around it. Your mind wants to immediately seek answers for what has taken place, but none of it makes any logical sense. Soon you come to realize that the truth is just truth, accepting the grim facts and learning to live with it.

The way to decipher whether truth is truly real for the highest good or what we believe to be true for our own emotional benefit is to recognize when a belief is being challenged. Typically when this occurs, it sparks an emotional response that may put you on the defensive side and you'll find yourself defending your belief. Before you speak up, ask yourself if this is in alignment with the big puzzle of truth. Because it could be Truth's devious little stepbrother named Denial. Denial is: *the action in declaring something to be untrue.* The key word is "declaring." We declare something to be untrue, or true, when in reality we are only making ourselves feel better as we align with the outcome of our choice. I say, deny denial. Denial is not our friend. It keeps us hidden, small, and insignificant and it intentionally hides us from the truth. Yep, I've got two magical words to follow that statement up: until now!

A student of mine made a profound statement that has stuck with me. He stated, "If I were to ask a crowd of 100 people, 'Who would like to see things get better in their life?' 100 people would raise their hands. If I were to ask the same 100 people, 'Who likes change?' a majority of hands would go down." We will deny, rationalize, and literally lie to ourselves to get out of having to change. However, if what you're doing isn't bringing you joy and happiness then it's time to stop rationalizing and begin realizing. Be honest with yourself. Our minds tend to create stories, "truths" of who we are, when in fact we are not truly recognizing who we are. It's difficult to see the truth in yourself, especially when you like what you see and don't "see a need" for change. This is the ego telling you that you're fine just the way you are. If this were the truth, chances are you wouldn't be reading this book. There is a part of you that feels a call to change. In order to truly make alterations to your life, you need to consider the fabric of the whole self. You've realized for one reason or another that change is occurring. You know deep inside it's time to change some aspect of your life.

If this resonates as truth within you, then it's time to look in the mirror and see yourself from a higher perspective. Remove all self-judgments and don't listen to the tapes playing in your mind from others' opinions or experiences. Stop telling yourself things like, "Oh I can do this just once because it's not hurting anyone or no one will know," or "I can have this candy because it's the holidays." Or, "This person may be bringing me down, but he has a good job and he provides for me." Thoughts like these are called rationalizations. These thoughts are not in alignment with your destined self. When you become aware of these self-sabotaging thoughts, you will begin to see a new you emerge. It's not easy, nor is it comfortable to change these thought patterns. After all, you've been telling yourself it's okay for too long. It's no longer okay for your mind to control your spirit with thoughts that don't serve your highest good.

Part of the Realize phase is connecting with the most authentic part of your self, where truth resides. When we finally remove the masks we've been hiding ourselves behind, something amazing happens. You begin to open up space for massive change to occur. Your newfound self-awareness begins to alter your thinking and pattern of behaviors to get the outcome you desire and deserve. When you remove this aspect of yourself, be conscious of the fact you may feel that void I was referring to earlier, almost like something is missing. It's like an unsolved mystery or a movie without an ending. I am here to tell you that's a good sign. You are officially moving into the next phase of transformation, which is Releasing. Take a few moments to discover the truth about yourself.

Self-Discovery:
- Define truth in your own words. What does truth feel like to you?
- What situation are you not seeing the whole truth in or are in denial of? (Age, relationships, happiness, etc.)
- When have you rationalized to make yourself feel better?
- What is the truest quality about your self? (Ask someone

who loves you if you are unclear.)
- When have you not been completely honest with yourself?
- What changes have you made in the past that you are really proud of? How did that make you feel?
- Create a timeline for your journey of transformation.
- Write down goals and achievable action steps.
- Meditation: Clear and open your mind, take a deep breath, and imagine a white feather of truth floating in the air; it holds the truth of your destined self. Just as it wanders around you, you hold out your hand and it lands in the palm of your hand. What truth did this feather bring? What new insights does this feather deliver?

Part 2

Release

The Second Stage of Transformation

Chapter 4

Align Your Allies (Relieve)

Now that you've conquered the Realize phase of transformation and you are beginning to remember the aspects of your best self, we step into the next natural phase of transformation, which is Release. This is probably one of the most difficult parts of personal transformation, as many times we don't want to let go of something that has been a part of our life. This is when faith steps up to the plate for you, picks up the bat, and swings at the ball you cannot see.

The story that comes to mind is the day I lost that wonderful opportunity that appeared in the darkest time of my life and literally transformed it. It was the leadership development project at a large communications company I had been a part of for nearly four years. I had played an intricate role in changing the corporate culture there and, based on the survey responses from the students, I was very successful in my efforts. In fact, I was asked to become the Lead Trainer for the rollout of the newest leadership program and would be responsible for training the other leadership trainers. It was an incredible opportunity. I would be working side-by-side with some great instructors who I considered to be my friends and was ecstatic about working together to make this next program highly effective.

Then out of the blue, I got a call and was abruptly let go from the project. What I learned was that another trainer felt rejected when she didn't get chosen for the project and therefore deliberately and viciously took me down. Rather than calling a potential violation of a company policy to my attention, which would have resolved the issue quickly, she took it straight to the legal department, which terminated my position instantly. My misunderstanding was clarified; I took personal accountability of the incident and corrected the issue immediately. But it was too late. I went from being the superstar to being a falling star by the simple act of a jealous, fearful, and devious person. This client was my "bread and butter" at the time and suddenly I was without an income. So you can imagine my disappointment, discouragement, and distress. I had never felt such betrayal in my life. Transformation suddenly kicked in once again.

Here is where the lesson really appeared. Of course my ego was severely bruised and its first reaction was retaliation. My emotions were now like a crazy rollercoaster ride, but because of my awareness of these phases of transformation, I immediately took the observer perspective, removed myself from the entire situation, and took the skyscraper perspective. I got a flash of the roadmap of my life and saw how divinely planned this occurrence was in propelling me forward. After time healed the wounds of betrayal, I actually reached out to this woman and thanked her for doing what she did. In fact, the day after my little pity party (I am human after all...I gave myself one day to dwell on it...that's all the self-pity energy I allowed myself), I did some yoga, meditation, and journaling. I noticed it had been a couple of months since I had written in my journal. What captured my attention was the last sentence from my last entry. It read, "Release all that no longer serves my higher self and purpose." "Yikes!" I thought to myself, "I created this?!" You bet. Spirit knew it was time to move on. The bus she was driving reached a fork in the road, took a sharp turn (on two wheels!), and began to accelerate down another unknown path.

Intentional transformation requires us to release whatever is getting in the way or keeping us in a comfortable place. I can honestly say that project was all-consuming, which didn't allow me much time to embark toward my destiny. Instead, it served as a stepping-stone. These invisible barriers that feel so comfortable and secure can prevent us from greatness. You may have heard the quote, "Life begins at the end of your comfort zone."

My story is proof of this. I know that project was my security blanket, which allowed me to procrastinate when it came to doing things that supported the highest vision of myself, which is to write, speak, and create positive change on a bigger scale. As long as I was getting a paycheck, I was happy. But the truth is, I wasn't completely fulfilled. The calling for me to fulfill an even greater purpose seemed to be waiting for me to pay attention to it once again.

Perhaps this event was the Universe telling me *it's time to move on, you have gained all that you need to gain from that experience and let's get you back on your path to your destiny.* It's like I was flying down the freeway at 70 miles an hour when suddenly I saw this barricade that read "The road is closed," and a huge sign with flashing red lights screamed, "Stop and Go This Way!" I recognized that this heartbreaking, devastating event was a huge directional sign, which forced me to immediately put trust and faith in my divine self that is connected to the Almighty Creator who essentially regulates the creation process. And so, I was reminded, I am not truly in control of what occurs in time and space but as long as I remain in the thoughts of my highest self, I will flow with the force that makes the grass grow and planets rotate. My experience has proven time and time again that when we are in *this* place, life moves with ease and all is provided for. After all, the trees, grass and planets don't feel the need to control the process of their growth.

You see, when we land on a soft cushion, we tend to want to stay there. It keeps us complacent and this is the phase of transformation where people tend to lose momentum. We unintentionally give up on our destined self and put it aside. Many of us are not willing to release what we have to in order to move into the next level of greatness. However, if we ask to release what no longer serves us and our highest vision, then we must be prepared to accept what shows up. The same goes for relationships and people in our lives. Something to be aware of is that when we release something or someone that has required much of our energy, it leaves a space, a void, and a feeling of emptiness. Knowing this is very important because this is usually when people go back to unhealthy relationships and old patterns of behavior. Just be patient during this phase of releasing and observe your journey. In time, you will begin to fill that void with positive, productive, and passionate energy. This will be explained in greater detail later in this book.

What my higher self knows for sure is that the woman who "threw me under the bus" and I had a special soul contract. She was simply playing out the role I had asked her to. It was done out of love and she has played one of the most important roles in propelling me toward my destiny. There is no other reason for her to be in my physical life; she served her mission within our relationship and so I release her with love and bless the power within her. All relationships have a purpose in our lives. It doesn't matter if it is a parent, sibling, friend, lover, boss, or a stranger at the grocery store. Everyone who enters your life is there for a reason. They enable us to learn who we are in the reflections they provide for us. Some relationships remind us who we are and some remind us who we are not. Either way, we learn from them, take the lesson, and move forward.

Here is what I have learned from this particular lesson. It's important that we recognize the messengers life delivers and make sure we are humble enough to receive the message they are delivering. It is most effective when we can remove ourselves from the situation and observe from above. What you've attracted so far is a reflection of your "story," who you were before you entered the Realize phase of your personal transformation journey. Be selective as to whom you let on your bus and who should be waving to you on the sidelines as you drive on by. Some people just are not yet equipped to go where you are heading. There is no need to discard people you love and care about—simply share your new approach toward life, lead by example, and trust they will follow when they are ready. This gives them the gentle nudge as you hold up the mirror, letting them look at themselves (through you) and allowing them to identify their own highest vision.

I am going to get a little "woo-woo" here for a moment and share a belief that I adopted along my journey. Through the study of Numerology I have become convinced of certain truths. I believe before we got to this place called Earth, we sat down with the Almighty Creator and we mapped out our lives; created every aspect of the lessons we came here to learn. Imagine for a moment that you and God sat down one day (prior to your birth) and wrote the story of your entire life. You got to choose your body, your looks, and your personality too. You both agreed on who would be your family and all the people you would meet here to be a part of your life journey. I believe you and God handpicked the messengers to help you remember who you really are and fulfill your soul purpose that God has intended and you agreed to. Some of those people have shown up already, but there will be many more messengers on your path. Pay attention to everyone who enters your world, every song, every sign, and every book. They have been placed there to help you remember why you are here and who you are, or in some cases, who you are not. Remember that people are usually a reflection of an aspect of you and they are just there to play the role you asked them to, all for Divine purpose. So forgive easily and often.

During this process, be aware that you will go through a phase of very few associations, and you may feel like you have no friends. You may experience isolation, seclusion, and perhaps some depression as you are re-aligning your associations. This is all perfectly natural. You will experience a subtle grieving period, which includes emotions like denial, anger, and finally acceptance. Know this so that you do not go back into an unhealthy relationship that prevents you from excelling. The emotional impact of changing affiliations is temporary but extremely powerful and necessary. As you observe your life, also observe who you associate with; ask yourself, "Are these people I admire, even have a little healthy envy for?" If the answer is yes, this is good. We usually see a reflection of an aspect of ourselves in those we admire. This is just an opportunity for you to see, through others, your own potential that has yet to be tapped into.

There are four categories of relationships that I put into four quadrants. The first category contains those relationships that empower, encourage, and support your highest vision. You usually walk away from these people feeling energetic, happy, and capable. These are healthy relationships to have in your life. You want to surround yourself with these people as much as possible.

The next category are those you admire, envy, and even judge. These are significant because these messengers are here to show you something about yourself that you may have forgotten or haven't noticed yet. This can be a healthy perspective on yourself or perhaps an unhealthy one. If we are envious of someone, not jealous (there is a difference—one is love-based and one is fear-based), then we wish to create in our lives what that person possesses. This allows us to reach for the stars and be introduced to something we would like to experience. That is a healthy perspective. Whereas, if you judge someone for who they are, what they do, or decisions they make, be sure to look at yourself first. We usually see faults in others because it's through an unfiltered perspective of what we have yet to deal with within ourselves. For example, if you were to say of someone, "She just gossips all the time," you are actually exhibiting that same behavior you're judging that person for. Pay close attention to these relationships, as they bring great insights on what to release during this very important phase of transformation.

The next quadrant is one that contains relationships that require much giving of your energy. These are the people in life who you support, encourage, and empower on a regular basis. The fact that you are helping someone may boost your energy temporarily, but after a while this can drain you. Your energy is an extremely valuable commodity and many times we pour our energy onto others more than we give it to ourselves. When we do this we empty our energetic cup, and having too many relationships like this makes it difficult to refill your energy cup. These types of relationships can create an extreme imbalance in your life. This is why it is so important for you to give to yourself first so that you have enough energy overflowing to give to others without sacrificing your own enlightenment.

The fourth category of relationships is what I call GTHO (get the heck out!). The "Ghetto" is no place for anyone to be. These relationships are destructive, can be abusive, and are very disempowering. In most cases, these people try to diminish your power, keep you small-minded, and discourage you from any growth whatsoever. Because the truth is, if you change that means they may have to change also, and for some change is way too scary to embrace. So these fearful folks will do everything in their power to make sure they are in control and prevent you from being a threat. This is the unhealthiest type of relationship one can have. It would be to your benefit to remove yourself from this type of relationship so that you may continue your journey of transformation and evolve into your next best self. Keep in mind that it may take some time to rebound from this type of release because it occupied so much of your energy and tainted your self-belief system. In the long run, you will be stronger and more secure, and you'll become highly self-sufficient once you get back into the flow on the river to your destiny.

There will be a time on your transformational journey when you may have to clean up your relationship circle and create one that better serves you. When you become intentional about who you align with, ensuring they resemble and support your highest vision, you will notice an acceleration on your journey to your destiny. Remember, mastery, or being dedicated to your destiny, is the road less traveled. If it were comfortable, everyone would be doing it. Take a moment to revisit your associations.

Self-Discovery:

- Re-evaluate your associations so they're in alignment with your highest vision of yourself. Make a list of your top 20 closest relationships.
- Who in your life disempowers you or makes you feel smaller than you are, only to make themselves feel more powerful?
- What people or relationships in your life hold you back from your greatest self-vision?
- Who in your life makes you smile? Who makes you cry?
- Who in your life empowers you, supports you as your highest vision, and believes in your potential?
- When do you put yourself around people or in positions that resemble your "story"?
- Activity: Create a Relationship Quadrant. Determine which relationships are *significant*, meaning they enhance your life, and which relationships are *productive*, meaning they produce positive results and support you in moving in the direction of your destiny. Create a private list of people in your life by placing their initials in the appropriate quadrant. This will help create the awareness of what purpose those relationships serve in your life.
  1. Empower/encourage/support me (Receive)
  2. I empower/encourage/support (Takes)
  3. I admire/envy/judge (Provides a healthy or unhealthy reflection of myself)
  4. GTHO—Get the heck out! (Energy "vampires" who literally suck the life out of you)

Remember, create awareness of all people in your life, align your allies with your highest purpose, and keep your relationships above the line!

Relationship Quadrant

	PRODUCTIVE	UNPRODUCTIVE
SIGNIFIGANT	People who empower, encourage & support me *(I receive positive energy)*	People I admire, envy or judge *(Provides either a healthy or unhealthy reflection of myself)*
INSIGNIFIGANT	People I empower, encourage & support *(Requires that I use my energy)*	GTHO—Get the heck out! *(Energy "vampires" who suck the life out of me)*

Chapter 5

Open Door Syndrome (Re-evaluate)

As you continue to move through the Release phase of transformation, begin to expand your awareness and open up to the insights highlighted in this chapter. Observe what resonates as truth and pay attention to anything that causes you to pause. I am about to uncover one of the most important lessons I have learned during my personal transformation experience.

People come in and out of your life for a specific reason; each one serves a purpose. They are all meaningful messengers. But it's something that must be monitored and controlled; otherwise, some who have a strong sense of purpose will try to take you with them on their journey rather than you fulfilling your own destiny. It makes it really hard to dedicate yourself to your calling when others are pulling you in another direction or are not supportive of your vision. When we open ourselves up to the types of relationships that distract us from our calling, our passion in life, we eventually become stagnant and unhappy and feel unfulfilled. Many times these types of relationships are camouflaged by something we call "love." Whether it be a casual friendship, family relationship, or romantic interest, we tend to rationalize our role in the relationship, while sacrificing our own purpose.

In my case and that of many other women I know, this behavior is the result of lack of acceptance in our lives. For whatever reason—perhaps it stems from not getting enough attention as a child, or being neglected in a previous relationship—we crave acceptance from the people around us, especially new people who enter our lives. This is what I call the "open door" syndrome. Because of the feelings of lack from your past, you open doors to people who often misread your intentions, instantly see your unmanaged emotional pain, and automatically move in to try to fix you. Their emotional dysfunction is attracted to yours, and this energetic connection is sometimes perceived as love. In reality, it is pain fueling pain. These types of relationships, if you are not aware, lead to more experiences of that pain. The same goes for your shining light, your smile and positive energy. Many are attracted to light for the mere reason of healing their own pain. Your friendliness might be misconceived and they may see the relationship as a romantic opportunity whereas you had no intention of going there. These are examples of the open door syndrome.

Having this awareness has helped me immensely to set specific boundaries regarding those I open the door to my life (and heart) for. Over time I have learned to open these sacred doors for those who are mutually beneficial, meaning we support one another on our paths toward our destiny. I have also learned how empowering it is to close the doors that sabotage our growth. Opening the right doors and setting proper boundaries with people takes you to your destiny much more quickly and makes the journey more pleasant.

So here is how to be your own bouncer at the door of your precious life: Observe. Assess. Choose. Observe when/who/what you open doors for. Truly be aware of the lesson, the purpose of this relationship; look at all potential outcomes. Assess the benefits for you and determine what they bring to the table for you. Also, because the more you give the more you receive, assess what you can bring to that person in return. Remember how important it is to balance the energies in a relationship. And finally, choose to find the category, or quadrant, of where that relationship fits into your world. Making good and wise choices leads to doors of opportunity. Poor choices lead you to nowhere. Be selective and trust the outcome will serve you when making these life-altering choices from your heart.

One of the most powerful tools I have in my Life Toolbox is

simply to learn how to say "no." I was that person who thought I could do it all. I had a difficult time saying no and always over-extended myself. There was a time in my life when I gave, gave, gave until there was nothing left to give. I often found myself getting depressed from lack of time for myself. I felt exhausted and unfulfilled because I was being pulled in so many directions. It takes great courage to say "no," but once you do, your spirit soars with gratitude that you have stuck up for yourself and reclaimed your power.

Here is a profound universal truth: "no" simply means nothing changes, life remains the same. When you say no to something or someone, your and their world doesn't change in any way. It is when your answer is "yes" that you alter the course of the future. Empower yourself by learning to say no and know when to say yes. Again, the way to remember is: observe, assess, and choose. Set those clear and concise boundaries and hold yourself accountable for sticking to them. Know the difference between a door of opportunity and a door that takes you back to your old story. This is a journey of transformation to a great version of yourself; if you don't change these types of behaviors, you will remain where you are.

When I changed this one behavior, things began to significantly change for the positive for me. I began surrounding myself with people who empowered me and were not just with me for their own benefit. Once you become aware of the doors you've opened, begin to gently close the ones that do not serve your highest vision. Some you may slam shut; others you may want to keep cracked open in case an opportunity does exist down the road. Either way, this requires some honest communication and humility on your part. I've had to have some uncomfortable conversations with some I considered good friends of mine, letting them know I was embarking on another path and that some of the decisions they made and behaviors they chose were not in alignment with who I have chosen to be. These friends remain in my heart forever, but I don't have to partake in their drama any longer. It is quite liberating, actually.

It is also important to make a conscious effort to reconnect with others who are messengers that have or continue to serve and support your purpose. Perhaps this means reaching out to those who said something to you that inspired an "aha moment" or did something for you that turned your life around. Just a simple thank-you for that act of kindness brings them back into your consciousness. What this does is create an energetic support system. You make them feel good by acknowledging their good deed, creating positive energy all around. Again, this type of conversation does require some courage, but let me tell you, it is so worthwhile on so many levels. I encourage you to find it within you to make that special and meaningful call. I truly believe we place certain people in our lives with great strategic insight, knowing they will deliver the perfect experience for us to evolve at that particular time on our human journey. They have a right to know how they contributed to your personal growth.

When making decisions about what to do or who to let on your bus ride to your destiny, you may be able to categorize people using these types of doors:

1. Revolving door—this is when you make the same choices and allow the same type of people into your life over and over again; one enters, another one leaves, still keeping you in the middle of nowhere. Nothing changes until your choices change. Stopping this is the behavior shift that will propel you to the next phase.

2. Sliding door—only opens from one side; either they let you in or you let them in, but seldom with mutual respect. Be very cautious with these relationships. One-sided relationships are energy vampires.

3. Swinging door—not clear on who is entering, you never know which way the door will swing, with people coming and going from your life. If this is an occurrence in your life, then it's time to set some strict boundaries. Get yourself a door-stopper and place it at the door so you can see and control who enters next.

4. Locked door—where you let no one in and trust very few people. These barriers limit your opportunities, and you stay stagnant because you're not willing to take any risks, or you may fear any type of change.

5. Basement door—when your door opens to people who bring you down; it lowers your energy and keeps you in the dark. Creating awareness of this type of behavior is the first step toward releasing this pattern, which will allow light to come into your life.

6. Rooftop door—lifts you up higher, takes you to a place where there is no ceiling, a feeling of limitless possibilities. Imagine you're on the top of a skyscraper; when you open this type of door to possibility, you have great perspective on your life and clearly see where you're heading and with whom.

Recognizing the types of doors you have in your life will help you to manage the "open door" syndrome. This is all about creating awareness. Once the awareness is established, change is already in motion. Allow it to proceed and do its job while you change the appropriate behavior or action so that the pattern is broken and you release those who no longer serve your highest good.

Self-Discovery:

- Draw a picture of a door (or cut one out of a magazine) and decorate it to show what you envision your new door to look like. This is your visual reminder of your beauty and worth, to help you remember to let in only those people who deserve to be in your home and share your valuable life.

- Ask yourself when making any choice, especially about the people in your life: does this choice keep me in the dark or does it bring light into my life?

- When have you opened doors for people who have kept you in Nowhere?

- Who should you not open doors for any longer?

- When did you open doors of opportunity? How did that feel? What was the outcome?

- What do you observe about yourself as it relates to opening doors in your life?

- What kind of people do you let in? What causes you to do this?

- What circumstances do you open doors for? What causes you to do this?

- Which type of door do you typically default to? What changes do you need to make, if any? How will this benefit you?

Chapter 6

Secrets, Fears & Tears (Reveal)

One of the most important self-dedications of the Release phase is outlined in this chapter. As you make the necessary adjustments that have been described thus far, it is now time to reveal your secrets, face your fears, and allow the tears to flow freely. This is how you free yourself from the feeling of complacency, lack of confidence, and incapability caused by shame and guilt. Past behaviors have led you to this place, but rest assured, you can clear the clutter and choose again. Because we are all in the human form, chances are you've done some things that, when you look back, make you feel an inkling of regret. Perhaps there were circumstances in your life that led you to make decisions you're not proud of. These may be in the form of choices you made, experiences you've had, or even perceived "failures" that you have swept under the rug in hopes to never deal with them again. But I've got two magic words to share with you...yep, "until now."

These thoughts of the past have been stuck in your psyche and eventually molded themselves into beliefs about who you are today. It's time to do an energetic lobotomy and take a look at what's under the hood. Since this body and mind are what carry you through this life, it is vitally important that you remove the "gunk" that gets stuck in the engine and prevents you from operating at your full potential. By lifting the rug, seeing all those things that you've been sweeping under there over the years, and shining the light on each one, they will begin to disintegrate. Shine the light on those dark secrets and fears, and watch them run like little mice.

I am not a trained psychologist by any means, but I share this information with great confidence because it's what worked for me. Once I released the untold secrets, faced the psychological fear, and allowed this debilitating energy to escape through my tears—lots of tears—life suddenly became brighter and I felt most empowered.

First, let's take a deeper look at fear. I am not referring to cautious fear, like "don't touch the hot stove or you'll burn yourself." I am referring to the psychological fear caused by untrue tapes that were recorded in your mind and now prevent you from greatness. It's time to play back those tapes, listen to them carefully, assess where the fear stemmed from, create an awareness around when that fear arises in your life, and wisely choose again. This is the process to follow every time you recognize fear stepping in to ruin your day: assess the fear, create awareness, choose again.

Now that we know how to move through fear, let's notice how it can appear in our lives and the damage it can cause. Fear can show up as a friend, but be aware because it truly is a disguised enemy. Like that annoying neighbor who just stops by out of the blue, unexpectedly showing up unannounced, and you're hesitant to let them in—and then you find out that neighbor is there to tell you the back of your house is on fire and they already called the fire department for you. There is always a reason fear shows up in your life. And in this case, it's to heal an unhealthy belief you have had about yourself that you've avoided for too long. Although fear is one of the most common reasons we make the choices we do, often we find we make the one that feeds the fear rather than making the choice that feeds love. Fear and fear-based emotions such as doubt, worry, guilt, and jealousy don't serve us. They keep us feeling trapped, insecure, and incapable. However, awareness of fear can be the wake-up call saying, "What are you going to do this time?" It's a golden opportunity to choose again. It's another chance to break the pattern of belief you've allowed to bully you for way too long. Realize that your past has helped mold who you have become—the good, the bad, and the ugly. Start by being aware of your past and observing the choices you have made; through that awareness alone, you will build momentum toward the change you desire. This is especially true when fear arises.

As you begin to recognize fear (you'll even taste it), you must immediately step into "observer" mode and see if you can check off any of the fears on this list below. These are the top 10 human psychological fears that prevent people from achieving their highest potential:

- Fear of rejection
- Fear of failure
- Fear of uncertainty
- Fear of loneliness
- Fear of change
- Fear of loss of freedom
- Fear of being judged
- Fear of getting hurt
- Fear of inadequacy or not being good enough

Think about choices you have made with any of the above fears in mind. Did you stay in an unsatisfying relationship because you really feared loneliness? Or did you avoid making a commitment to someone special because you feared losing your freedom? Did you supposedly turn down that promotion because it meant more travel but really there was just a fear of change? As you begin to think back to certain turning points in your life, realize how those choices may have changed your course. Making decisions from fear tends to take us off the path of our destiny. It's taking risks in life and trusting in the unknown that truly liberates us.

Once you have established those fears—and perhaps it's a pattern that has occurred time and time again—now it's time to get to the core of what the fear is (being as transparent and honest as possible), and then shine the light on it. Fear is like a thief getting interrogated at the police department with the big spotlight shining on its deceiving face; you stand behind the two-sided glass observing its reaction as it reveals the reason why it wanted to steal your roadmap to success. It's fear's job to do this. Where did this thief, or belief, come from? What life experience did you have that rooted this belief in your mind? Or was it someone else's fear that transferred to you when you were young? Dig deep and know this: it's all made up. Fear is an acronym for False Evidence Appearing Real. Fear is built by believing something from the past that isn't true. Fear is part of the illusion in life, the stories we have told ourselves. Sometimes we even pass on these fallacies to others. It will be worthwhile to take time in this chapter's self-discovery section to dig up those ugly weeds in your garden of truth.

I have been battling fear-based emotions that resulted in self-doubt for as long as I can remember. Not many people would know this, however. I have always been confident on the outside, but internally I wasn't so self-assured. I had many self-sabotaging beliefs that showed up as worry, and fear of not being accepted. These beliefs were what motivated many of the unhealthy choices I made as a young adult. I recognized this pattern because the same type of people and situations kept showing up in my life. So here is what I did to dramatically alter my pattern of beliefs from when I was a little girl. I have become relentless at recognizing the first signs of fear appearing in my life. I now know how to replace fear-based emotions with high-vibrational feelings. For example, rather than worrying about money, which consumes much of one's energy, be curious about where the money will come from next. It is a powerful exercise that will manifest good things instead of more fear. It's a practice, but one that will certainly change your brain chemistry, give you a more positive attitude, and surely assist you on your journey.

Let's shine the light on your secrets, shall we? Did you feel some discomfort when you just read that? Good, then we at least know you're human with real emotions. You are human and are entitled to err. However, when you make a conscious choice to be dedicated to your destiny, this entitlement dissolves. After all, that is why we are here, to learn who we are and who we are not, through the choices we make, actions we take, and outcomes at stake.

Once you make a commitment to yourself to avoid behaviors you'll be ashamed of in the future, you will no longer live a life of secrecy, meaning you will have nothing to hide. You will crave clean living and that, my friend, is freedom. In order to clear the path of your destiny, you have to avoid the potholes (shame and guilt from keeping secrets) that keep deflating your tires. When these potholes are repaired the road becomes smoother, and so does life. When you recognize the secretive, deceptive, low-vibrational energy of secrets you've kept, it begins to bring a new perspective as you look back in time. You begin to understand who you were then, and see that it really didn't serve you well; you can gain the lesson learned, release it once and for all, and finally heal that part of your life.

Secrets are like a ball and chain; energetically they hold you back from fulfilling your highest version of yourself. It's time to live life outside of the closet, time to come to terms with who you've been, release that part of yourself, and begin to reinvent who you know you are destined to be. You may have done things you wish you hadn't before you knew what you know now. That is okay. Don't beat yourself up for it, for that will use up some of your valuable energy. Give yourself ample time to work through this phase and process what could feel like a rollercoaster of emotions.

It's never too late to make a fresh start. We get to the core of our destined self by peeling back those layers that fear built around us. Fear wanted you to believe it was protecting you, but in reality it was building a wall that now you have to break through to get to where you want to be. Acknowledging *all* of your secrets is a must in order to free yourself, not just the ones that are the easiest to deal with. Take ownership of your choices. See how they have created a pattern that has not served you and how they may have hurt others. These secrets are not just yours after all, they're all of ours, and when you hold that negative energy in, it alters your authenticity and truly impacts the people around you.

Here is the big picture: those deep-seated secrets that are left ignored interrupt the natural process of humanity, which is unity, closeness and oneness. When we feel shame from hiding our past, this prevents us from living in harmony with one another. It can destroy relationships with people you love as your innocence that connected that relationship is gone and that circle of trust has been broken. You can try to hide it or push it aside as if it never happened, but know that your authentic self will never show up until you dissolve these secrets. If you are ready for your destiny, then now is the time to do just that.

In my experience, this was one of the hardest things I had to do. And when a good friend of mine recognized and cared enough to shine the light on this shadowy energy I carried around, life suddenly became more fluid, meaning it started flowing freely. Doors began to open, my messages were clearer, and a very strong sense of personal empowerment motivated me to continue on this path of clean, clear living. I was reminded that "character is what you do when no one is watching." It's not that I wasn't ever living with good character, it was just that when it comes to certain times of my life I can say, "I wouldn't have done those things if my dad was watching." This has always been my guiding thought prior to making decisions. I would ask myself, "What would my dad say about this?" There were times I failed to answer that question, and this resulted in making some poor choices that may not have been in my best interest. Well, now, as I embark on this journey to truly authenticate myself, I have had to work through this energy that I carried with me all those years.

What worked for me is forgiveness, transparency, and humility. There is a tremendous amount of power in self-forgiveness. Forgiving yourself and others releases the anger and feelings of remorse and regret; all those emotions that hold us hostage, keep us emotionally crippled, and reinforce our old stories that keep us in the darkness. This is easier said than done, however. Self-forgiveness is not just saying the words, "I forgive myself." It's honoring yourself for being human. It may be that you have to repeat those words until you feel them in the depths of your soul and you realize this event is part of your human experience. You will know when you do because tears will fall as if to release this bottled-up energy, like shaking a bottle of soda that eventually pops the cap off. This is what you have to do, shake it out of yourself until the pressure builds up so much it explodes. Spend some time in the self-discovery section of this chapter to really shake things up. It's important you do this before moving on to the next phase, which is Rebound. You need to clear this energy to make space for all the good stuff you are about to create for yourself.

There is no greater leadership characteristic than humility. To be humbled is to be your most authentic self at the core. We demonstrate this inner self by being transparent in what and how we communicate, how we think and express ourselves. It begins with being honest with ourselves and recognizing our thoughts, words, expressions, and reactions to certain outcomes. At times, we tend to allow our egos to flare up and take control. When this happens, our authentic self goes away and hides. However, when our authentic self is in charge and doing all the talking, our egos will take a back seat and follow its lead. Others will be automatically drawn to someone who is humble, honest, and transparent. Transparency is when we are speaking so honestly that people can see through us. When they do, and see there is nothing to hide, you then will know you are on the right path. There is a deep connection and understanding between human beings that occurs when we communicate at this internal level of honesty. It does take courage to admit our wrongdoings and poor choices, because our egos many times won't allow us to; these are the layers that need to be peeled back, one at a time.

The question may be arising in your mind about now: "Do I need to literally make a confession to the person I hurt or may have deceived?" The answer is no, absolutely not. If you made a choice that could potentially hurt someone if they knew the truth, it is not necessary for you to be truthful with them as much as it is for you to be truthful with yourself. The root of the behavior was made by the choice you made. This core is where the release and forgiveness needs to occur. Otherwise, you will continue to make the same poor choices and continue to hurt more people with your behavior. It's the behavior that needs to change so that keeping secrets, which is the outcome of your action, will no longer be a part of your existence.

This is your life story; you get to decide what character you wish to play and when to begin playing that role. It starts with a simple vision and a choice. Choose wisely. You've got some work to do, some very internal and personal soul-searching to explore. I tell you this: When you do this important work, it will be the most rewarding thing you can ever do for yourself. Wipe the slate clean and begin to live the life of your true self, one that leads to your destiny where all your dreams come true.

Self-Discovery:

- What secrets do you have that have prevented you from living out your dream?
- What did it feel like when you had this experience? (Guilt, shame, self-satisfaction, regret, etc.)
- In a private setting, make a list of all your dirty little se-

crets—the big ones and tiny ones.

- Begin to take ownership of each one by reading them all aloud in first person ("I lied to my parents, boss, friend, etc.," "I was unfaithful to my spouse," "I cheated on a test in school," "I caused damage to my body by doing drugs," etc.)
- Then authentically apologize to yourself. You are really saying sorry to your spirit. Your spirit is who you truly are whereas your mind (the decision-maker) simply made some poor choices for whatever reason felt good at the time. So it's time for your mind to admit its wrongdoings, own them, and release them.
- What was your mind rationalizing to make it "okay" to do these things?
- Then say aloud, "I forgive myself for cheating on that test in school," etc. Repeat until it's felt deep within your soul. You'll know it is released when you begin to cry. Crying is the body's way of releasing emotional energy. If you can't cry, you're probably not yet willing to face it and let it go. This can take time to accomplish, so perhaps revisit the exercise every day. After all, this energy has been a part of your story for many years. It takes tremendous courage to face these little demons that have held you back from your glory.
- What does it feel like to let this secret go once and for all?
- Once you have come to peace with yourself, say a prayer of gratitude, meditate, or just sit in silence to honor this moment of transformation. Be pleased with yourself.
- Exercise: Write your secrets on a piece of paper, put them in a box or bag, choose one at a time, read it aloud, proclaim self-forgiveness, then tear it up and destroy it, turn it into confetti, toss it in the air, and celebrate releasing this former behavior.

Part 3

Rebound

The Third Stage of Transformation

Chapter 7

Revive Your Spirit (Recuperate, Rejuvenate & Rebalance)

By now you have created an awareness about or are already working on releasing much of the stuff in life that has held you back from being your extraordinary self. Whether it was an unhealthy relationship that needed to be released, self-sabotaging thoughts, or a destructive pattern of behavior, chances are you have put some heart and soul into this phase. You may be feeling some unfamiliar emotions as you begin to process these impactful changes in your life. It's important to understand that once you release any aspect of your life that has been a part of your story for years, maybe even a lifetime, it will leave a void in your life. You may feel an emptiness, a loss, or even loneliness. It is important that you work through these emotions and allow time to grieve, as that part of your life is no longer.

You may feel apprehensive about your choice to release those energies, disappointed that you are not where you want to be, or simply sad as if someone or something you cared about has died. This is all very normal and a natural progression toward the next phase of transformation. Knowing this is very important so that you are not tempted to go backward and begin making those same choices again. This is where many people return to that comfortable complacent place, despite knowing it's not beneficial on the journey to one's destiny. People often go back to those unhealthy relationships or old patterns of behavior because they didn't allow enough recuperating time.

When recuperating from what may have been massive change in your life, be sure to nurture your body and manage your stress. I could write an entire book on stress management. I will just share the basics with you so you can create an awareness around how stress impacts your life. Stress is the internal response to an external event, called a stressor. When we can identify the stressors in our life, we can get to the root cause of most of our stress.

Your body is the vehicle in which your energy travels during this life, and how well you take care of your body will greatly impact how quickly you reach your destination. Ways I maintain healthy physical energy: chiropractor, blood type diet, Tabata, yoga, dry skin brushing, deep breathing exercises, smiling, good posture, water, apple cider vinegar, probiotics, organic diet, low sodium, low sugar, lots of water and fresh foods.

1. Self-love: Practice self-love—the only way to find true love
2. Self-kindness: Be kind to yourself—you'll find people will be kinder to you
3. Self-nurturing: Nurture yourself—keep your cup full so that you can fill up others
4. Self-honoring: Honor your journey—celebrate the successes, learn from the failures
5. Self-trust: Trust yourself—so that you become trusted
6. Self-knowing: Know yourself—who you are and who you are not

What prevents us from living these natural laws? By now, you have begun to realize some of the barriers preventing yourself from experiencing these natural and healthy habits. The only thing that prevents us from loving ourselves is not giving enough love. The only thing preventing us from being kind to ourselves is that we are not kind enough to others. We don't nurture ourselves enough because we give too much of ourselves to others. We may not honor ourselves because, until now, we haven't had the proper self-awareness of the creative power we have in our lives. We haven't trusted ourselves because we don't trust others. These are fear-based thought patterns that may need to be re-evaluated. Finally, we don't know ourselves because we haven't taken the time to do so. We haven't observed ourselves in the reflections of others enough to see the amazing creatures we are. We have spent too much time comparing and competing, and not enough time compassionately caring for others. We have created a self-absorbed society, obsessed with how we look, caring way too much what others think of us with little focus on our interior make-up, our inner beauty, truth, and goodness. It is time to stop the madness, contribute to a healthier society, and demonstrate for others the true meaning of beauty. People will stop in their tracks and do a double-take when they look at you and feel that radiant energy reflecting back at themselves as if to remind them of their own beauty within.

The fact is, the "security blanket" of whatever it was you released in the earlier stages is easier than the anticipation of the unknown. Fear of the unknown is like kryptonite to Superman: it can strip us of our power if we allow it. That is why it is so important that you embrace these next chapters and marinate in the messages that will guide you toward filling that empty space. The chapters that follow contain all the insightful ingredients you'll need to get past this restful phase and begin to taste the delight of your destiny.

Self-Discovery:

- Practice self-love: Every day, give yourself a hug or look in the mirror directly into your eyes and repeat these three powerful words, "I love you," until you feel it.
- Practice self-kindness: For just one week, sit in silence for 5 minutes each day. Think of all the ways you are kind to yourself. Practice these often.
- Practice self-nurturing: Indulge in inspirational movies, videos, books, etc. This will nurture the soul. Nurture your body by eating healthy foods and drinking lots of water.

- Practice self-honoring: At the end of the day, remind yourself of each success or any progress you made. Celebrate by lighting a candle to reflect and honor your own light.
- Practice self-trust: Try something you have never done before or have avoided. Breaking down fears builds trust.
- Practice self-knowing: Describe yourself in three words. Write down everything you have learned about yourself within the past month, 1 year, 5 years, 10 years.

Part 4

Reinvent

The Fourth Stage of Transformation

Chapter 8

Live Regret-Free (Reprogram)

How cool is it that no matter how much we feel we have messed up our lives, we can still have all the do-overs we need? Once you have released the guilt, regret, shame, fear, and all those negative-based emotions that hold us back, it is finally time to press the "reset your life" button. This is where you begin to reprogram your thinking and pattern of behaviors. Again, all change happens with awareness first. You've done this by holding up the mirror and seeing what has occurred in your past that is not in alignment with your destined self. You have begun to let go of previous behaviors, and now it is time to create new habits for yourself, a belief system that supports your destiny, and thought patterns that will create a positive outcome. If you have worked through the self-discovery exercises in the previous chapters, those changes are well underway. Think of it as tearing down an old broken-down house; now you have a clean foundation on which you can begin building your new structure, the home of your dreams. Now you get to pick out the upgrades and design your new self so that you become that showcase house on your block that everyone slows down to admire.

It is true, we all have a past that may not have served us well. You may have done what you wish you hadn't, or didn't do what you wish you had. Either way, you're okay because you are in the process of releasing these energies. I will tell you what I have shared with many students of mine: "Don't 'should' on yourself!" (Be careful when saying that out loud.) Let that word be a part of your past. It doesn't serve you in any way to say, "I should do this" or "I should have done that" or "I shouldn't have said that." You get the idea. It's a waste of your valuable energy and thought power. Moving toward your destiny involves

74

changing your language so that it empowers you and does not sabotage your hard-earned growth. It is vitally important that from this point forward you become aware of your word choices and begin to speak with certainty. In the table I provide some examples of what I like to call "Leadership Language."

UNCERTAIN WORDS	WORDS OF CERTAINTY
Should, would, could	Can, can't
Might, maybe	Will, won't
I hope, wish, want	I am confident, know, trust
Unsure, uncertain	Absolutely, certainly, positively
If	When

As leaders in life, we are now responsible for speaking with words that hold us accountable. Our words are golden. There is an energy behind every word we speak and that energy is a representation of who we are. I have taken words like "hope," "wish," and "want" out of my vocabulary because they are not specific enough to describe what I am creating. When I say, "I will follow through" on something, it sounds more confident and certain than when I say, "I hope to follow through." It's like when someone says, "I will try to call you tomorrow." Chances are I will not hear from that person. My point is, it is crucial that at this Reinventing phase you become aware of your self-talk, as your development is at stake. Your words can either accelerate your journey or slow you down.

If you are not getting what you want out of life, then perhaps you have been "wanting" things to happen. When we want things to happen, many times we get more "wanting." When we say, "I will have this, or I will do that," now we are getting somewhere! It's time to speak with absolute certainty or not say anything at all.

Also, to live regret-free is to learn the power of acceptance. If you dwell in the past and continue to marinate in remorse for choices that got you where you are, you will never move forward. Acceptance is the action of consenting to receive. It is time to receive and allow what you have always hoped for to enter into your life. Before you can allow these wonderful things to miraculously flow into your life, you have got to come to terms with your past. All of it. The good, the bad, and the ugly.

Here is what I learned about my journey once I had the rooftop view from the skyscraper I reinvented for myself. I saw every path, every choice, every option presented to me at those times when I was at the fork in the road. For example, I was living in Los Angeles as an aspiring actress in my early twenties. Opportunities had begun to present themselves—and then I met my future husband. This was a major turning point in my life and I chose the path of a simple family life over stardom. Many times, I would look back and regret this decision. I would try to integrate both paths, but to no avail. I now see that no matter what choice I made at that time, that path would bring me to the same place in time. For whatever reason, neither family nor fame felt fulfilling.

From my rooftop perspective, I saw the point where both paths met; this was the time of my "awakening" and so my spiritual journey began. Without regret, I began to seek my highest self and purpose in life, my destiny. I accepted my journey and my choices and realized I do have the power to choose again. I accepted that it is not what I do in the lifetime that matters, it is who I am being and who I continue to become. Would I have loved to have that experience of being on the big screen? Absolutely. But like anything else in life that is not rooted in our true self first, we end up taking it for granted. It's like the new car you have always wanted. It's exciting for the first couple of months, then it just becomes a vehicle that takes you from here to there. The decision to have that new car was not rooted in a higher purpose; it was a temporary fix in search of happiness. I read a sign recently that said, "If the grass looks greener on the other side, perhaps it's time to water your own." It is so true. Once you have that awareness I keep mentioning, of knowing when you desire something outside of yourself, that is the time to look within to see what is missing. What is missing is what calls to be nurtured. If your intention for that new car was to bring you a new image, then perhaps it's within yourself that the new image resides.

Know you are on the right path. All the paths lead to the same place. It's our free will that enables us to choose which path to take. The outcome is directly determined by whether you choose that path from a fear-based emotion or a love-based emotion. Either way, you will get to a point of realization that there is more to life than what you have been experiencing. As I mentioned earlier, these points typically show up as events; some are subtle, others are more drastic, but either way they are life-altering points in time. Whatever is happening in your life right now is part of the divine order to get you to your destiny. Accept the experience whatever it may be, as it is a compass here to guide you in the right direction. This compass is truly a gift from God, so accept it as such. Find gratitude as you learn to accept the change that is occurring in your life, knowing it is showing up to take you to higher places. These events are what build the walls of your new building. They must be strong and sturdy and so must you as you continue to rebuild yourself.

The beauty in all this is that you will always have the freedom of choice, your free will; you can always choose again, 'til the very end of your human life-journey. No one is making you stay in a place of sadness and discontent but yourself. What fear is keeping you there? Find it, face it, and eliminate it. Then choose again. Soon you will begin to make better choices that are in alignment with your higher self, and the feelings of discontent will dissolve.

To help you make these choices, ask yourself this question: "How would this make me feel if I were looking back on my life at age 99 while swinging on my front porch swing? Would I re-gret it or not?" Analyze the situation but especially pay attention to the feelings that show up. See what is preventing you from moving forward. Don't rationalize and be sure not to let fear and self-doubt sway your decision. If your spirit is calling you to experience this, and it's in alignment with your higher self, then go for it—you will never regret it!

As long as you have a pulse, you still have time to do what you've always wanted to do. Time to get creative and think out of the box. When you're in that creative space, let your imagina-tion go wild and listen to the inner voice that speaks to you. The thoughts that enter your mind are those of your higher self; pay close attention and then take action. Spirit will guide you gently, knowing that baby steps are required before you can take leaps.

At this stage of the game, it's important to know what is driving any decision you make. Self-awareness is your greatest friend right now. Begin to recognize those actions that are based on fear-based emotions like doubt, shame, guilt, etc. Remember that fear is just an acronym for False Evidence Appearing Real. These ideas show up from those old tapes that play in our minds, planted by other people's fears and doubts. When we allow fear to lead us, we are only betraying ourselves. The message we are sending to the Universe is, "I don't trust myself enough to move forward with my dream, so I will choose to be distracted in-stead." This is fear at work.

What distracts you from being productive? I have found that I clean my house as a distraction when I really want to be writ-ing or creating my next training program. So now when I begin cleaning, I have to stop myself and ask, "What am I avoiding?" Self-discipline is a topic we will cover in a later chapter. Right now, it's more important to learn to create the awareness of be-haviors stemming from fear and self-doubt so we can stop them before they take us down the path of self-destruction once again. To break through the barriers of fear and self-doubt, first you must recognize when they show up. Usually this is a pattern of thinking or behaving, a fractal. You have to reprogram your way of thinking about yourself. This is the perfect opportunity to apply the "UNTIL NOW" principle. When those unhealthy patterns appear, say something like, "I once allowed fear to distract me by cleaning my house...until NOW."

Now, I recognize fear and immediately choose to do what serves me, whether it be writing, creating, or meditating. Set those fears and regrets aside once and for all. Realize that back then you acted on instinct but now you know differently. Now you act intentionally. Be sure to ask yourself when taking action, "Is this choice I am about to make based on instinct (past behaviors) or intention?" Do you feel guided by God or guilt? All of these decisions lead to experiences and help to define who you are and who you are not. Our experiences are lessons and growing opportunities and as you may know, the deeper the pain, the greater the lesson. Only awareness can cure those wounds and prevent further emotional injury. You've got this!

Self-Discovery:

- What opportunities did you miss because of fear or being too afraid to try?
- What opportunities did you miss because of self-doubt, not feeling good enough?
- What lessons did you learn from this?
- How have these lessons served you on your journey?
- How can you achieve these opportunities in your life now?
- What is the greatest regret in your life?
- Where did your journey take you from there?
- What were the blessings in taking that route?
- Sitting on your porch swing, looking back on your life at age 99, what do you see yourself doing at this current age that makes you proud?

Chapter 9

Create a New Story (Redefine)

"Bloom where you are planted." I love that statement! I used to think that if I only had certain things or lived in a certain place, then I could be happy. I was in constant pursuit of happiness. The irony here is that happiness *is* the pursuit; it's never a destination, at least while we are in human form. Unfortunately, I had to learn this lesson the hard way. I thought if I wasn't married, perhaps I would be happier alone. Although I felt more free being single, I cannot say it brought me more happiness. I thought moving to my hometown would bring me comfort and happiness; it didn't. I believed that if I had a certain job and made more money, then I could afford things that would make me happy—but when I had the amazing job with the hefty paycheck, it required much traveling that took me away from my son, and I soon became highly stressed being away from home. Although this job put my financial worries at ease, the money certainly did not generate the happiness I hoped for.

I made several choices in my pursuit of happiness that, now that I can look back, actually created more stress. When that stress finally caught up to me, I had to, once again, look at myself, reassess my life, and create a new story of what happiness truly means to me. What I have learned, and the message I am sharing with you today is: the only place to find true happiness, and authentic joy, is in your passion, your purpose, your destiny. All other perceived feelings of happiness are merely a facade that fades in time, a momentary glimpse at joy. It's when you find your true mission as a human being that inner peace and happiness become an effortless, natural state of being.

This is truly where the fun begins. Now that you have cleaned the slate, you get to rebuild your life the way you choose, knowing what you now know about yourself. And because you have cleared out much of those energies, emotions, and fears that prevented you from being happy and feeling fulfilled, you will find yourself smiling for no reason at all. I remember the day when the clouds lifted out of my life, when I stepped out of darkness and into the bright light of day. I had been doing this work you are reading about and one day when I was walking my dog at the park, I noticed I was smiling. I had to touch my face to believe it. I observed this shift in energy and literally asked myself, "Where have I been?" I noticed myself feeling lighter. The weight had somehow been lifted and I could feel joy radiate through my body. Normally, I would walk and worry about my future or analyze my situation. It wasn't until this day that I realized those thoughts while walking were patterns of behavior that needed to change. And through my self-discovery work and releasing of many of the other behaviors, this one presented itself as clear as day that it too had been released. So now, I walk with intention to be inspired, I admire the nature around me, watch the people, and listen to the messages that appear in my mind. When small shifts like this begin to happen in your life, you will know you are making progress. And when you become aware of this progression and can celebrate the smallest little success, then you will know the space has been cleared for you to begin reinventing yourself.

As you begin to awaken your natural state of being, allow your spirit to guide you to rediscover what it has in store for you. This means transferring all of your decisions from your mind into your heart. When it comes to finding happiness and living your destiny, it is important that your choices be made from your true self and not your mind or ego. So be careful here, or you will slip back into places you've already been. If you focus on what your new story *feels like* rather than what it will look like to others, you will know you are allowing your spirit to drive the decision. Ask yourself, before making choices, "How will I feel about this decision one month from now, one year from now, or ten years from now?" This will be your guide. Trust me, I have made some choices, and if I had asked that question each time, I wouldn't have to write a book about how to overcome poor choices.

Here's the thing: you have full creative rights over your own life story. Most people know this, but few practice it. Your story is a piece of this Grand Illusion called life; a compilation of everyone's story makes up what the world is in this moment and what it will become in time. How you create your story will have a direct impact on the world, whether positive or negative. The energy you produce from your state of happiness contributes to the energy on this planet. We can see by watching the news the horrific energy that consumes some people, and it can spread like wildfire onto others. So does your vibration of happiness. The better your story, the more it impacts the betterment of the world.

The one thing you need to realize about your story is this: you're making it all up. I mean, listen to the drama you hear others talk about. It's their viewpoint being projected onto others. I love the work of Byron Katie. She asks the famous question, "Who would you be without your story?" And, "What would my life look like without this situation?" When you can answer these profound questions, you begin to step out of that place of victimhood and into a place of authenticity. You truly begin to see yourself outside of the story you have been telling yourself, whether it's the story of your childhood, your relationship, or your state of happiness. It's time to tell the story of truth, the story that aligns with the reason why you chose to be here, and stop wasting your valuable time and energy on senseless conversation and thoughts. Perhaps this perspective will grant you some immediate peace of mind: *Life is a precious privilege, a temporary existence that allows us to experiment with living a highly impactful and influential life.* You may want to marinate in that one for a moment or two.

In this Reinvention stage of transformation, you may notice your thoughts drifting to the past. As you reflect back, you may feel yourself longing for those simpler days. Be aware when this happens so that you don't drift into sadness or depression because your life now appears to be lacking those things. The truth is, those moments were not as joyous at the time as they are looking back on them. This is part of the story you are telling yourself. If you continue to tell yourself that you were happier back then, you will continue to dwell in the past, and those thoughts strip the joy from this amazing moment.

So, it's time to manage these thoughts. Set an intention for yourself to recognize when these types of thoughts occur. This is the mind, the ego, knowing itself based on the tape recordings it's been told over years and years of programming. It will take time to rewind these tapes so that you can record your new story. Allow yourself time, and be gentle with yourself as these past memories may pop up out of nowhere. You have done some clearing and so the mind has to generate thoughts, that's its job. It's the job of your spirit to delegate which thoughts you will allow your mind to now produce. There is so much power in thought management. There is even more power in awareness mastery. Managing thoughts and mastering awareness around your own patterns of belief is what will accelerate your transformation. You don't like the way you feel about yourself? Good! Choose again. These changes are a practice until it becomes a permanent pattern. This will be an ongoing process as you evolve through each phase.

Expand your belief system to include a high-impact life and vision of yourself. Make a promise to yourself. Keep it simple and stick to it like you would if you made a promise to your child or a best friend. This builds self-esteem and confidence and empowers you, gives you strength to take on greater challenges in life. These are the miracles in life we so often overlook. When we heal ourselves of misperceptions of who we think we should be, we begin to believe the untold truths of who we truly are. The miracle happens during this moment of acceptance of the higher truth. The guilt and shame is instantly released the moment you commit to making the choices that serve your spirit.

A couple more tips on recreating your story: be careful not to describe yourself with one of your human titles as an identity (boss, mom, dad, sister, CEO, etc.). These titles define who you are in relation to others, but they do not define who you are in relation to your highest self. Remember your highest self is one with the Creator of all things. Those human titles literally limit your story. They describe your human roles only. So be careful not to put a lot of energy in those titles, because they will change—whereas your highest self, which remains title-less and indescribable, will always be who defines you.

Sharing your new story often puts it immediately into practice. Others will notice a change in you when your actions change. You may notice that some people may not want you to change. As you reinvent yourself, know that not everyone will join you in the next chapter of your life. You can still love them from afar. So when I say to share your new story, be sure to share it with those who support and lift you up, not those people who fear you changing.

This is an important phase in which to apply the "UNTIL NOW" principle. Beware of the moments that will tempt you to fall back into your "old" self. Certain opportunities will appear during this phase to give you the chance to decide who you choose to be. Over time you will choose that which will represent your highest self and this will become your new normal. Your behaviors will determine the truth, and your emotions will be your guide. If you happen to fall off the edge and revert back to old behaviors, it's okay. You can still reinvent yourself. In fact, sometimes these times only solidify your destined self. Each time you feel yourself reverting back and you recognize those feelings, this means you have become aware that this circumstance no longer serves your highest good. As you are recognizing the conditions or outcomes made by your own choices, your story is underway—and although there may be some emotional discomfort and uneasiness, know that this truly means you are becoming a master of your destiny. Celebrate these moments... they are epic.

Self-Discovery:

- What self-sabotaging thoughts do you repeat about yourself? (This job stresses me out, I can't seem to lose weight, I'm always tired, etc.)
- When do you experience self-doubt? (Around certain people, in crowds, doing certain tasks, etc.)
- How have your current self-image, thoughts, and beliefs prevented you from living a highly impactful life?
- When have you felt like a victim of circumstance? Looking back, what lesson came from that experience?
- What part of your life have you created (by believing it was true) that has served you well? What was the specific behavior that triggered that experience?
- If you were to write a book of the story of your life, what would it be titled? What is the pinnacle or turning point? How would the story end?
- In your journal, write down any revelations you may have had around your awareness of unproductive thoughts, time, or energy.

Chapter 10

Become Your Observer (Reacquaint)

Welcome to the last chapter of the Reinventing phase of transformation. The strategy outlined in this chapter is the most important aspect of intentional personal development. The ability to know yourself is so powerful. This is when you know you're on the path to destiny, the way it was intended from the beginning. Our Creator made the trees, grass, planets, and all the beauty on this planet, but that Creator had a greater desire, to create something that would know itself in all its glory. Thus, the human being was born and with that so was free will.

At the risk of being too philosophical, I am sharing my personal opinion of my spiritual beliefs. As a society we have let our free will get out of control. Look at the destructive choices being made in our world today. We sit on our sofas and easy chairs, watching the news on television as if it doesn't affect us. We observe the world, say it's gotten crazier, and then we go about our lives as if none of it is happening. Many times, this is what happens with our own lives. We will only stop and observe our lives when a catastrophic event occurs to wake us up from the dream we've been living in and force us to look at ourselves, our lives, and our existence. If it weren't for these major turning points, we would continue to walk around this planet like zombies... yes, the walking dead.

There comes a time on your life journey when you suddenly realize you've been asleep at the wheel. You're not sure who's driving the bus, where it's going, or why. This is the awakening of that higher perspective and most importantly the observer. It's when we start asking questions like, "Where have I been?" that we know we have officially moved into this phase of Reinvention. This is the first sign that you are beginning to recognize your true self as you begin to observe your own transformation. Brace yourself for some major "aha" moments and "sudden truths" that will begin to appear. This is an absolutely magical place where you begin to realize why certain tragic events and catastrophic changes took place in your life. Be sure to practice deep intentional breathing during this phase, as you are releasing the build-up of energy from years past. It's finally time to let it all go and see yourself in the new light. Watch your wings unfold as they flap in the wind for the first time, preparing for your launch into the world like a beautiful emerging butterfly or a firefly flickering its light for all to see.

You are now transitioning from Seeker to Observer. A true observer recognizes the Seeker's transformation; honoring them for where they are, celebrating where they've been, and reinventing who they'll become. It's an interesting time, during this phase, to reacquaint yourself with...well, yourself. You have changed so much; the emptiness inside is less of a loneliness and feels more like serenity, a deep connection to something greater than yourself. You have accepted your journey at this point, you've done the work to get yourself here, and now it's time to pause and re-engage with the new and improved You!

I hate to use the word "accountability." It just sounds so corporate to me. But this is one of the "bilities" (as my friend Michelle Roebuck calls them) that require your personal dedication. In order for you to be capable of moving into the next phase, you must first be accountable for the actions that will get you there and the beliefs/behaviors that prevent you from moving forward. And in order for you to be accountable, you must first be reliable. Learn to rely on yourself for everything. Trust your thoughts, instincts, and intuitions. Have faith that you will and can be, do, and have anything you've ever wanted. This is why you are here, after all, to express your ultimate creativity in the likeness of our Creator, the living force within all of us. We can only take so much credit for our ideas and creations, for these truly belong to our Creator as the originating source of all thought. Our role as an expression of that Creator is to put them into action and deliver a manifestation of that creative force to others. This is the accountability part. We not only need to hold ourselves accountable for following through on the creations that come through us, but also hold God accountable for supplying us with the never-ending thoughts pouring through us that take us to our next level of evolution. By holding God accountable, we surrender ourselves to that incredible creative energy. All we have to do is quiet the mind, observe each and every thought that enters our consciousness, and remain in the present moment to allow that thought to manifest into form. It's not only a powerful process but one of the laws of the Universe.

Much like gravity, a force that cannot be fully explained, so is the Law of Attraction: *that which is put out into the Universe will be returned.* There are plenty of resources that cover that topic so I won't elaborate. The point I want to make is this massive creative energy stems from the electric power of each thought. Then, when that thought triggers an emotional response, that energy magnifies itself, giving the manifestation momentum. This phase is truly where miracles begin to happen. Each small miracle that you observe and appreciate is like a magnet for more miracles to happen. Begin to see the beauty in everything. There are no mistakes, no coincidences, only creations, and that creative power is within you. Use it wisely and the rewards are abundant. Do not let your circumstances define you any longer; recognize the excuses and eliminate them by practicing creative thinking.

It is so important during this phase to set time aside to get to know your new, true Self as if you were nurturing a new friendship. Make a date to sit in the park or take a walk in nature with yourself. Literally, put it on your calendar as "self-time." This can be a period of self-reflection and healthy isolation. You may start to crave alone time as you begin to self-discover a healthier you and re-establish new boundaries for yourself and in your relationships. You will slowly begin to build a healthy relationship with yourself and make each part of yourself a friend and ally. Understanding all the "allies" that make up your entire Self and creating the self-awareness around each aspect of these "allies" will increase your self-esteem, confidence, and most importantly, self-love. These "allies" are present physically, emotionally, spiritually, mentally, personally, physiologically, and psychologically. Observe them, monitor them, and even document your findings to learn more about this amazing being that is finally making its cameo appearance into the world.

How do you create an alliance with yourself? It can only be done from the perspective of your higher self, by observing yourself and continually learning who you are by asking yourself tough questions. Then listen closely to the answers that appear. Ask yourself questions from the sidelines like, "What is it about this relationship that fulfills me?" "What am I grateful for in this moment?" or "How can I become even more aware of my patterns of thought and behavior?" Questions like these will keep your mind stimulated and your spirit alive. A simple understanding that the observer is your spirit, the decision-maker is your mind, and your vehicle to get you from Point A to Point B is your body, will create clarity to let you become more consciously aware of your destiny and purpose. Moving to the passenger seat every once in a while will only build momentum toward your destiny like a stone being washed and tossed by the flow of the river—it becomes smoother and smoother.

Now is the time to climb up to the rooftop and take a top-down or bird's-eye perspective on your life, your behaviors, your choices, your relationships, your outcomes, your thoughts, and your feelings. While you're up there, notice the streetscape, landscape, and beauty of your journey. Look at where you've been and see where those choices are taking you. Recognize the behaviors that have changed for the better and celebrate your successes, even the tiny little breakthroughs. By doing so, you give yourself permission to change, and fear begins to dissipate as confidence builds. It's about being of this world but not in it, as Jesus said. This is where you really begin to honor all of your three parts: your spirit, your mind, and your body.

A couple of things to be aware of (and I learned this the hard way): make note of when the observer is your spirit and when it's your mind (ego). To know the difference, understand that spirit will make observations that are aligned with a feeling of gratitude, such as how your kindness helped others, or how you made a difference, or what the impact was on another person. Ego, on the other hand, will want to see you as the "great one," which feels more like, I am the one who made that difference, the "good person" who did that act of kindness, or the "brave one" who impacted that person. There is a fine line, but you will notice a particular charge when the ego is dominating. It wants you to believe it is why you are doing all these great things, but it is not what is truly driving you, it just wants the credit. The ego is not a bad thing, as long as you are aware of its presence and are able to manage it when it becomes too domineering. This takes practice and some major self-awareness training.

Spirit's best interest will always be emotionally charged with love, unity, generosity, and compassion. It's easy to identify when spirit is driving the bus, because when you observe your journey you will see the light in others and how much brighter it is because you flickered bright enough to ignite it. Whereas ego will believe *you* ignited their lights—it's all because of you. Ego will observe from the perspective of fear (I must be better than others), competitiveness (I am the most generous person in my group because I made a difference), separation (I am a better person), and self-serving gratification (I did that, wasn't that amazing?). When your perspective begins to shift in this way, you must stop it immediately. If you allow your ego to take all the credit, your spirit cannot thrive. And it is your spirit that is calling you to your destiny. Your ego is of the mind, which is thought-based. Thoughts are implanted from outside sources, previous experiences, or future visions. Therefore, ego takes you out of the present moment and into the past or future. It doesn't hurt to visualize every once and a while; in fact, when used to set healthy intentions, it can be very powerful. Just know your true path to destiny will only be guided by your spirit, which knows why you took this human form to begin with. And there is only one place to find spirit—and that is in this exact present moment. Your presence is a present, unwrapping the gift of true prosperity.

Self-Discovery:

- Self-inquire often and self-discover the inner you daily. Journal: what did you learn about yourself today?
- What are 10 (or more) ways to spend valuable time with yourself?
- When will you schedule self-time?
- Schedule self-time events and put them in your calendar for the next year—this is a way of life; you'll find you will see the benefits of self-time and it will become a necessity. Examples: *Bike ride every Saturday morning along the river bike trail from 8 a.m. to 9 a.m. Take a candle-lit bath each week. Engage with the children in your life, on a regular basis.*
- What successes can you celebrate today?
- What are 10 ways to celebrate your successes?
- Schedule time for self-celebration on a weekly basis. It's okay to bring people into your celebratory moments, especially the ones who support your growth.
- Which one can you relate to the most, the butterfly or the firefly? Why?
- Answer the following questions as your spirit observes your life from the rooftop; make note of the feelings that accompany these answers.

A. What does society dictate you "should" have, do, be, etc.?
B. What are you most proud of as you look at where you've been?
C. Where do you see your path leading next?
D. Is there anyone joining you on parts of your journey? If so, who?
E. What was a situation you wish you would have handled differently?
F. How would you handle that situation now, knowing what you know?
G. What decisions are you facing?
H. What is the potential outcome of all of your choices?
I. What are the changes you are now aware of that need to be made?
J. What beliefs no longer resonate as truth?
K. What are your beliefs or thoughts that replace those old beliefs?

Part 5

Resurrect

The Fifth Stage of Transformation

Chapter 11

Manage Your Energy (Remain)

As we move into the next phase of transformation, and begin to Resurrect to our highest self, we must fully understand and have the foundational belief that everything in life is made of energy...everything. The planet is one huge ball of energy in constant movement, and we are made of this same magnificent metaphysical mystery of the unseen that continues to be studied and better understood by scientists. This giant ball of energy was formed from the energy of the Universe, and life began to emerge from this energy. Humans are made of the same energy; we grow hair, the Earth grows grass and trees. We are made of about 60% water, and the Earth is about 70% water. Mother Earth is undergoing transformation, impacting the energies of her human species. She experiences extreme weather patterns (natural disasters such as tornados, earthquakes, tsunamis, floods, etc.) and we experience transformation that feels like a severe storm, hurricane, or tornado, where life spins us around into a dark vortex of gloom. That is, UNTIL NOW.

Now we are able to lift ourselves up (hence the Resurrect phase), put ourselves back together (balancing the spirit, mind and body connection), and learn from the gift this life-altering event delivered as we become humbled by the miracle that has shifted us forevermore. Knowing how these transformational energies operate will enable you to use this incredible force to your advantage. Much like the Earth, which has energy vortexes (a vortex is a place in nature, like in Sedona, Arizona, where the Earth is exceptionally alive with energy — a place where the Earth energy swirls and draws to its center everything that surrounds it, like a tornado), we have chakras (the seven centers of spiritual power where energy exits and enters the human body).

Being a student/teacher of yoga has given me great insight into monitoring each of the seven chakras in my body so that when I feel weak in a particular area in my life, I can focus on the blockage of energy at that chakra. When I clear these blockages, that life force then begins to work within me, effortlessly and limitlessly. There is so much information on the topic of chakras available today. So that you have a basic understanding of these energy centers in your body, here is a brief description of the seven human chakras:

1. **Root Chakra**—Our foundation. When activated, we feel grounded. Located at the base of our spine in the tailbone area. The emotional impact: survival issues such as financial independence, money, and food.

2. **Sacral Chakra**—Our connection, our oneness, and ability to accept others and new experiences; the umbilical cord of life. This chakra is located in the lower abdomen, about two inches below the navel and two inches in. The emotional impact: a sense of abundance, well-being, pleasure, and sexuality.

3. **Solar Plexus Chakra**—Our personal power, our ability to be confident and in control of our lives. This chakra is located in our upper abdomen in the stomach area. The emotional impact: self-worth, self-confidence, and self-esteem.

4. **Heart Chakra**—Our ability to love and be loved; our openness to love. This chakra is located at the center of our chest just above the heart. The emotional impact: love, joy, and inner peace.

5. **Throat Chakra**—Our ability to communicate; our voice and importance and ability to be heard. This chakra is located at the throat. The emotional impact: communication, self-

expression of feelings and the truth.

6. Third Eye Chakra—Our sixth sense, our ability to focus on and see the big picture. This chakra is located on our forehead between the eyes (also called the Brow Chakra). The emotional impact: intuition, imagination, wisdom, and the ability to think and make decisions.

7. Crown Chakra—Our connection to Source, this highest chakra represents our ability to be fully connected spiritually. This chakra is located on the very top of the head. The emotional impact: inner and outer beauty, our connection to the source of imagination, creativity, and pure bliss.

Becoming aware of these energy centers in the body will help us maintain a healthy vibration. When you begin to notice a physical ailment in the body, say in your digestive system, take some time to listen to the message your body is trying to deliver. The message may be that you need to step more into your own power. If you begin to encounter a sore throat, you may need to step back and ask yourself, what needs to be said and to whom? The more we understand our own energy and how to manage it within our bodies, the more healthy we become physically, emotionally, and spiritually. And the bonus is that we begin to feel the oneness with all that is on this amazing place called Earth. When we connect in such a profound way, life becomes balanced and we begin to proceed through life with ease and grace as if to flow with its natural current. Your life has changed in some way, and with change comes an energy shift. Pay close attention to these waves of energy levels, as you wouldn't swim in the ocean when the tide is high and the current is forceful. There are forceful energies during tides of change. You can either be pulled down by the current or learn to flow with them to accelerate you to the shore of your destiny.

You have experienced these energy vibrations I am referring to, like when you are feeling sluggish and tired and emotionally heavy, and sadness, depression, or some other fear-based emotion is creating stress, discontent, and heartache. These energies drain us of our life force, whereas those higher-energy vibrations that give you a pep in your step and a sense of enlightenment and empowerment, such as acceptance, trust, appreciation, and love-based emotions, are what create harmony and true prosperity.

Learning to manage your energy so that the vibration remains in the Destiny Zone is the most important action you can take to master the Resurrect phase of transformation. I love this quote I heard from Brendon Burchard: "The power plant doesn't make energy, it generates it." Which means you are responsible for manufacturing your own positive energy. You can no longer depend on outside resources to raise (or lower) your energy levels. Here is a brief snapshot of Energy Management training tips I can give you, based on what worked for me in my own experience:

- Become accountable for where you spend your valuable energy every minute of every day. Are you doing things that are productive and in alignment with your vision, or are they distractions that take you away from your purpose?
- Manage your time. I recommend studying Stephen Covey's Priority Quadrants to help categorize where your time is being spent. Time is the only commodity that cannot be regenerated. It is our most valuable asset if we use it properly.
- Have a solid Stress Management Plan. Stress is an internal response to an external event. Change is the culprit of all stress. Change and life are synonymous. Recognize the symptoms of stress and have a plan to eliminate its effects.
- Clean out your spiritual or energetic closet. Be aware that

you may feel some residual energy from your past, and regrets may creep in from time to time. Revisit the Release phase of transformation to identify what still needs to be worked through.

- Keep your energy clean. Muddy energy caused by kept secrets slows the process of becoming your greatest version of yourself. You must clear that energy by looking at the issue and taking responsibility for coming out of hiding. Your behaviors must be in alignment with your higher self from this point forward. These truths must be realized and released.

- Practice forgiveness regularly and release blame. Forgiveness is the cure to the negative energy that you've accumulated. Releasing blame prevents negative energy from building up. True freedom lies in releasing blame. There would be no need for forgiveness if blame did not exist in your life. Bless those who have crossed you or disappointed you in any way. It may be people you've never even met who stress you out and cause a negative energy shift. For example, crazy drivers on the road. Why allow them to lower your energy vibration when you can raise theirs by sending them a blessing or sending them light to protect them and people around them as they drive irresponsibly? You really do have this power.

- Be aware of "energy vampires." These people may not know they are feeding on your energy because they haven't yet learned to generate their own positive energy. If you find yourself feeling tired around certain people, teach them so that they can learn to manage their own energy. Many times, we encounter people with negative energy and their energy transmits to ours, only to ruin our day.

- Acts of kindness are a tremendous energy-booster! Compliment someone, surprise someone, be generous for no reason, empower or encourage someone, tell someone "I believe in you," or send a random note to a friend or family member. Your connection will enable you to engage with their emotional response when they receive that message that will in turn raise your energy level, too. This is a great way to keep the second chakra open and clear to receive the same energies.

- Focus on what you want, not what you don't want. These intentions will place your energy in the buckets of what you want, preventing you from pouring your precious energy into what doesn't serve you. When a situation does occur that is not in alignment with my higher purpose or destiny, I quickly put the Focus Factor into place to release it and move into Redefining myself:
  - Figure
  - Out
  - Cause (your why)
  - Understand
  - Solution (your how)
- Protect your energy. Make sure your vibration is strong and sturdy so that it cannot be tampered with. Energy work can be done anywhere, anytime, and doesn't need to be done in solitude. The only requirement is your imagination, a clear mind, and internal focus.

Remember, all these events causing a negative reaction in your energy have occurred because it was just part of your old story anyway. You created it, therefore you can clear it.

Learning to manage your energy is the most beneficial action you can take toward a healthy lifestyle. I will share with you a technique I have adapted from those I consider to be Masters whom I have studied with. This is what works for me, and so it is just a suggestion. I encourage you to find what works for you and become the master of that. All I know is that when I learned to manage my energy, everything changed for the better. I didn't experience as much of the rollercoaster ride and my mood was more balanced. As I learned to clear negative energy, I also noticed a stronger, clearer voice, which is energy vibration being formed into sounds and molded into words. I began speaking from my diaphragm, my lower chakras, a place of power. I also experienced a deeper feeling of inner peace and calmness and noticed I was becoming more immune to stress.

There are many ways to clear your energy; here's what has worked for me:

Stand, with feet planted firmly on the ground, hip-width apart. Take three deep belly breaths, inhaling deeper with each one. With the fourth breath, begin to imagine the energy from the Earth entering your body from your toes, up your legs, and through your torso and abdominal area, clearing each energy chakra as it travels through your body. Allow that energy to flow up around your heart center, your throat area, around your face, your third eye (between your eyebrows), and up through the crown of your head. Allow that energy to flow about two feet above your head before it begins to flow out and around you like a beautiful fountain of light. (As the energy flows around you it creates a high-vibrational force field, protecting you from negativity.) As the energy flows downward to the ground, bring it below the Earth's surface approximately two feet, then up through your feet again. Repeat the process until it travels so quickly your body can hardly contain the energy.

The second part of this exercise is to do the same thing, but bring the energy through your breath from the "heavens," starting at the crown of your head, down until it goes out your toes into the Earth approximately two feet, then up around you like a reverse fountain of light.

Once both these are clear and vivid, move the energy in both directions simultaneously. When you become advanced at this energy technique, you can begin to swirl the energy around your entire body like a cyclone going upward and downward. This builds a protective shell around your chakras so that the energy is maintained around your being and can only be dispensed at your will.

This energy work is especially important for those who wish to perform positive change in their world that involves other people. People of lower energy vibrations feed off of the higher vibrations of others, so whenever you go into crowded rooms or environments where the energy may be lower than your natural vibration, it's imperative that you protect yourself prior to entering. Create a cocoon of white light around your body and you will radiate onto others without exhausting your energy supply.

Self-Discovery:

- When you go into public with large crowds of people, how does this impact your energy?
- When you are alone for an extended period of time, how does this impact your energy?
- When you are around people whom you believe to be your supporters, how does this impact your energy?
- Why is clearing your energy important to you?
- When you did the energy-clearing exercise, how did you feel before the exercise and how did you feel afterward?
- What was the biggest challenge of doing the exercise?
- What can you do to get the most benefit from doing an energy-clearing exercise?
- What are some ways you can manage stress in your life? (Massage, meditate, play golf, talk to a friend/mentor, etc.)

Chapter 12

Commit with Purpose (Respect)

As a human being, committing with a purpose will keep you feeling alive and awake. If we don't have a basic understanding of our natural responses to life, then it will be difficult to change the course of our path. To make a commitment to yourself is the only way to sustain this level of transformation, this higher state of consciousness and enlightenment. When you evolve to this level of transformation, it comes with a responsibility. That responsibility is about making a pledge to entrust yourself to the collective good of humanity, beginning with your circle of influence.

Why is it so important to make a commitment to yourself? Imagine if everyone lived to the capacity outlined in this book. Imagine if everyone was living authentically and following their true purpose. Imagine what the world would be like if we all were on our path to our destiny and fear no longer played a role in our lives. Imagine the inner peace we would identify in each other's eyes. Imagine how that peace would illuminate the planet. This vision doesn't have to be a figment of our imagination any longer. We can begin living it and begin living it now... before it's too late and our time runs out.

It is our responsibility as a human to better the world we live in and become the highest version of ourselves. When we do this we not only honor ourselves, we honor God. After all, this life is the gift God has created for us. Doesn't it make sense to return the favor by giving our Source the gift of living the best life possible? When we do this, we radiate pure love, which is our natural essence. And love heals all. Love is what this world is in desperate need of today. So we must not hesitate, not even for a moment, to consider the importance of our dedication to destiny...for our good and for the good of all.

The best way I know to accomplish something I set out to do is to set solid goals. Professor Dr. Gail Matthews at Yale conducted a study that showed 76% of participants accomplished goals if they wrote them down, prioritized them, created action steps, told a friend, and reported weekly updates on their progress. Only 46% accomplished goals by stating them and never writing them down. So your chances of getting what you want out of life are great if you follow these steps! Start small but think big! Begin with a 30-day, 60-day, and 90-day action plan. Revisit your plan daily and weekly, putting it in your calendar for easy reference.

Make decisions/choices that are in alignment with what you want so you'll stop getting what you don't want. For example, if you want to get in shape, make a commitment to yourself to exercise daily. Start with just a 5-minute workout to start building that momentum, then the next week do 10 minutes, then add cardio the following week. No one says you have to begin with extreme urgency; when we do, we often fail, because we didn't have a plan and so we gave up. "Plan your work and work your plan!"

Being diligent about sticking to following your destined path is not always easy. You'll find, if you haven't already, that it is the road less traveled. Many people do not jump on this path in life. So I commend you for getting this far. There is one piece of advice I will tell you that truly works: don't just want it — command it! Call it into your life on a daily basis. This is the time to BURST out into the world and soar higher than ever before. You are building momentum now, so it is important to maintain those good choices that are in alignment with that higher vision. The last thing you want to do at this point, after all the work you've done, is to go backward.

Be aware that past behaviors will continue to show up and disguise themselves in tricky ways. If you are not in control of it, those opportunities to be your "old self" will keep testing you. Another responsibility you have is to maintain your current state of being. Sort of like an addict or alcoholic who needs to be aware of avoiding alcohol and drugs and the people who encourage them, you must use caution in this phase and every phase, for you may revert back to your old ways at the drop of a hat. Something can trigger you and spark an old feeling, perhaps an emotion you haven't quite worked through completely. These emotions can and will erupt. These stages of transformation are part of the reprogramming of the spiritual DNA; addictive behavior becomes predicted behavior. Those special messengers and teachers in your life may get frustrated with you during this regression, but you must stay on track to your destiny. As long as you are in human form you are a work in progress and those who love and support you will continue to love and support you as you continue to grow. Continue to be aware of your behavior as the observer, keep your word, and make a promise to yourself.

This is the phase of disciplinary action. It's time to OWN your life and be the living example of your highest self. This naturally gives people in your circle of influence permission to do the same for themselves. Trust me, people will notice when you begin to change and they will want to know what has caused you to become so confident and committed. Just keep believing in yourself as I believe in you. I have learned from polling students in my leadership training classes that most people have never heard these four special words spoken to them: "I believe in you." You can be the one person who says those four highly impactful words. Share a heartfelt "I believe in you" statement whenever you get the chance with someone, especially a child. They will remember you for that forever.

Self-Discovery:

- Practice believing in yourself. Literally look in the mirror, look yourself in the eyes and say the words, "I believe in you," until you feel it in your soul.
- What are you committing to first?
- What is your daily plan to get there? Weekly? Monthly?
- Schedule your monthly planning day each month for a year. Put it on your calendar.
- What behavior will you change first? (Put this in your Power Up People! app daily.)
- Taking the first step will be ultimately beneficial because...
- Write down goals, post them, read them aloud daily.
- Share with a friend and report to them weekly or monthly on the progress of your action plan. Who will I choose to share this with who can hold me accountable?
- How does this build momentum on my journey to my destiny?

Chapter 13

Dedicate to Destiny (Resolve)

The time has come for a resolution. Being resolute is having determination. If you haven't by now become determined to follow your destiny, perhaps this is the chapter that will put you over the edge. And by that, I mean take a running jump off the edge of your comfort zone and leap into the unknown, knowing your wings are ready to take flight and glide you toward a soft landing at your destined life. The edge is where true transformation resides. We love living on the edge, for it gives us the ability to see the horizon and all of the choices we have before us on our path. It is on the edge of enlightenment that we feel the most angelic support, our full capabilities, and a knowing of the ultimate trust. The edge is where we understand why we are here and trust that the steps will appear when we lift our foot off the ground.

For so long I was caught up in the "whats" of life. What will I be when I grow up? What do I want to do? What do I need to be happy? What. What. What! Then I discovered that life truly lies in the "why." Why I do what I do. Why I allow distractions to deviate me from my mission. Why I feel the way I do. Why I feel a certain way. All these questions of why became the core of my destiny. When I shifted from what I needed to be doing to simply embracing why I was doing it, life got easier and things began to flow at a quicker pace, almost as if I was airlifted and carried along the path toward my destiny. I no longer needed to exert any more energy that left me short of breath because of all the "whats."

Instead I focused on my "why." Why do I feel it to be necessary to help people navigate change so they become the next best versions of themselves? Why do I feel so passionate about activating the life force on this planet so that humanity is reminded of the love that they are? Why is it so important to me, to the point where I have released most of my "normal" life, to fulfill this mission, this calling, this destiny that tugs at my soul? The truth is, I could analyze it until the cows come home but I know the answer is as simple as can be. It is my essence. It is why I chose to be in this body with this mind and in the physical world.

Once I realized that this is my soul, my pure energy, my true self being expressed, I began to just focus on the feelings. How I want to feel is more important than what I am supposed to be doing. You see, when I focus on, and actually tap into, the feeling of peacefulness, that feeling immediately becomes my reality. When I focus on feeling prosperous, I am abundant in that moment. When I focus on feeling generous, I feel like I have more than I need and appreciate how good it feels to be able to give to others. When I focus on the feeling of satisfaction from empowering another person, I feel that I am on the right path in life. It is in these feelings that true transformation occurs. This is what my destiny feels like.

When we begin to feel our way to our destiny, the Universe responds with the "whats." It is not up to us to put in our orders of what we want; rather, dedicate yourself to how you feel. The next step is to open yourself up to receive what shows up. Your free will gives you the ability to choose your next steps, but trust that what is showing up is for your highest good and is there to carry you to your destiny. Be what you wish to become. As Felicia Searcy once said, "The world doesn't give us what we want, it gives us who we are."

I am here to remind you that you are not here by accident. You chose to be here at this time for a reason. It is time to follow through on your purpose. When you practice your daily meditation, practice feeling what your destiny feels like. Take time daily to envision your future self. Maintain that vision with a high level of awareness until it becomes a habit, and proceed with that vision without hesitation! We generally trust what we can see as opposed to what we can envision. I invite you to trust your vision. It is real and it is why you are here. Know it is truth and it is possible. Feel it in the core of your being. The world is desperately crying out for you to walk your path. Walk it for the people who don't have the courage, who have yet to awaken from their sleepwalking state of being, who have yet to discover their passion in life. Run, don't walk, toward your vision, embrace the growth that accompanies you, and choose to prevail no matter what. This is your time, your destiny, and it is for all of our good.

Self-Discovery

- What is your "why"?
- Imagine your life three years from now. Describe your relationships, health, your life professionally, emotionally, spiritually, and monetarily in first person narrative ("I am now...").
- Take a moment to feel what each of these feels like:
  - Prosperous
  - Generous
  - Curious
  - Certain
  - Experienced
  - Grateful
  - Peaceful
  - Harmonious
  - Grounded
  - Accomplished
  - Pleased with yourself
  - Satisfied
  - Loved
- In your journal, list the emotions that best describe your

destiny.

- What distractions do you need to be aware of?
- What are you doing that is forcing the river rather than flowing with the current of life?
- How dedicated are you in this moment to living your destiny? Rate your dedication level on a scale from 1 to 10 (1 = not feeling very dedicated, 10 = committed to living my destiny).
- What do you want or need to focus on daily? For your mind? For your body? For your spirit?
- How can you minimize the distractions while staying focused?
- What behaviors will you focus on to continually reinforce positive outcomes?
- What will you do today to achieve your future-self vision?

Part 6
Respond
The Sixth Stage of Transformation

Chapter 14

Build the Bridge (React)

Have you ever had one of those dreams where it felt so real, you could have sworn it really happened? My experience of one such dream was more than just an alpha-state of illusion; it was more like a crossover of two dimensions. It was a two-part dream, an extremely vivid and realistic dream. The kind where images of that dream remain in the forefront of your mind for days. There didn't seem to be much meaning to it…that is, until it crossed into my physical world and became known as more than a dream; it truly was an invitation from my destiny.

The vivid scene was me riding in the back seat of a touring van that was traveling along the edge of a mountainside road. The weather was gloomy and cloudy. I was looking outside the window as we drove along this unknown place in silence. There was a tour guide driving the van who seemed determined in his destination. I was alone on this trip, although there were others on board. I continued to observe the surroundings out the window over my left shoulder. I could see through to the other side of the mountain, and there were the most amazing white structures built into the cliffs. The lights from these breathtaking buildings glimmered through the foggy air. I could not take my eyes off of the beauty that nearly brought me to tears. This is when I awoke. I remember feeling the awesomeness of that place. The view is still very clear in my mind to this day. The realness of this dream struck a curiosity within me that caused me to research and explore what this magical place could be. Needless to say, I could not find a place on Earth that compared to its magical, mystical magnificence.

One week later, I awoke from the second part of this dream. I was still riding in the back of the van looking out the window, and the tour guide indicated we would be stopping off at a "lookout point." I was so excited I could hardly wait to get out and see what I could see. I walked to the edge of the cliff and, through the fog, tried to see those beautiful clusters of structures along the mountainside. Just then, I heard the voice of the tour guide behind me. A male voice announced to me, "There will be a bridge." Somewhat startled, I answered with an interested enthusiasm, "Really? What kind of bridge?" He described in great detail the white stone architecture and the tall arches that would support it. "It will begin right where you are standing." I listened intently as I imagined his description of this beautiful bridge and replied, "That bridge is going to be amazing, I am sure!" He continued, "And it will all be built by hand."

This is when I really became inquisitive. "By hand? My goodness that will take some time. Where, may I ask, does the bridge take you?" His profound reply was, "From one world to another." And in that moment, it made perfect sense as I recalled my glimpse of the white mountainside city as being a part of another world. He continued to speak with a serious tone in his voice: "This is why you are here; you have been selected to build the bridge." My mind did not fully comprehend this invitation, although I was flattered to be honored with such a request and responded, "Really? I am honored but I have never built a bridge before." He replied, "The instructions will be provided. There are a couple of guidelines to be aware of." With great curiosity, I asked, "What would that be?" He said, "You will have to leave this world behind and dedicate your lifetime to building the bridge."

In astonishment I stood there in full disbelief that this was happening. I turned around to face the tour guide and to my surprise no one was there. I began walking back toward the van and saw a silhouette of a person standing there. It was my former husband, Bryan. I said, "Oh my god, Bryan, did you just hear what he was saying?" He said he hadn't heard any of it. In a fast-paced voice I reiterated, "He was telling me they are building a big, beautiful bridge; it starts from this point and takes you from one world to another. He said I had been selected as one of the people to build this bridge! The only thing is...I will have to leave this world behind and be on that bridge the rest of my life." In a monotone, matter-of-fact voice he replied, "Sounds like something you can't pass up."

Then I awoke. I lay in bed in absolute awe at the realistic and vivid nature of that dream. It felt so real. I wondered why I needed Bryan's permission and then it occurred to me: I had always struggled with maintaining our marriage while traveling my spiritual path. He's always known this, and his wise soul clearly was here to provide for me and support me while I gained enough courage to embark on the journey of my soul. It was our soul contract being fulfilled.

This dream stayed with me for days, with lucid recall of all the graphic details. To clarify, this was happening during the most stressful part of my transformation cycle. Bryan and I had separated for the last time and I was struggling to maintain my peace of mind while managing a new traveling career and being a single mom. The only thing that kept me sane was my yoga practice, a half-assed meditation practice, and journaling my frustrations. Until one day, shortly after I had the dream, when I was journaling. I will sometimes channel messages from God-knows-who and write them down, only to make sense of them later. This day, before I could even put the pen to the paper, the voice was loud and clear: "Have you reached a decision yet?" I looked up and around the room in a panic, thinking someone was in the house! I actually stood up and looked downstairs from the loft where I do my yoga to see if my dogs had heard or seen anything. They were relaxed and calm.

The voice continued, "The bridge. Did you decide to accept the invitation to build the bridge?" I sat in amazement for a moment and said out loud, "That was real?" The instantaneous reply came: "Yes." I threw in my objections as if I still needed to be sold on the idea: "I understand I have to dedicate the rest of my life to this mission. I already feel alone, I am not sure being secluded on a bridge is the best thing for me." The voice answered, "There will be others. Others like you." I was still not fully on board so I added, "And I am okay with leaving this shitty, stressed-out life behind, but I will not leave my son." The voice replied, "You won't have to, as he will also build the bridge when he is ready."

It was in that moment I broke down into a sobbing cry of absolute humility. I realized what was being asked of me, and the direction of my human life. I understood in an instant the need for a bridge that allows human souls to cross over from a world of self-destruction toward one of indescribable exquisiteness and splendor. I understood the request and the gravity of the mission before me. I asked for some time before I would agree to accept the mission. After all, it is not every day you are asked to release your current life for an unknown one.

This decision haunted me day in and day out. I could not think of any reason not to accept. I know this is the reason my soul took this body, and when the human fears finally subsided I was ready to answer the call. I turned this moment into a ceremony of celebration. With candles lit all around, I finished my yoga practice for the day with the intention of writing my acceptance for the mission in my journal: "Yes, I accept the mission to dedicate my life toward building the bridge for humanity, and all that no longer serves this mission may be released." I could feel the angels dancing and smiling. I felt an enormous relief and at the same time an anxious anticipation for what was to come.

Since then my life has undergone the transformation I describe in this book. The Six Stages of Transformation were discovered through the process of following my destiny and so now it is your turn. I invite you to join me on the bridge. Those who are ready will come and those who are not will show up when they are. And let me remind you that you don't have to know what you "need to do" to build the bridge or "how" you will do it, simply "why" you wish to be part of this sacred design. When you remain in that place, the "what" and the "how" will appear. Ask yourself, "Why would I build a bridge to transform the world?" What are the issues happening around you that cause despair? This is where the bridge begins and it's up to you to lay down the first brick within your circle of influence.

There are a lot of lost souls walking around this planet, and building the bridge is the responsibility of those who have awakened, arrived at a certain place of acceptance, and acquired enough wisdom to look back and see where they have been. They know where they are going but are not attached to any outcome, concerned only that their behaviors and actions are in alignment to building the bridge for humanity. It is time to reflect for others their potential when they have forgotten and hold the mirror up for them so they can see their own magnificence. You just may be the alarm clock in someone's life, so that when you share your story they resonate with you and therefore relate to their own lives, and you can provide them comfort, support, and inspiration as they wake. They have been pressing the snooze button for years because no one has ever taken the time or effort to see them for who they truly are...until now.

Once you have received a sense of knowing, you now have a responsibility to transfer your knowledge and wisdom, and share your journey of how you got from *nowhere* to *knowing*. It's time to team up and help people navigate through the human experience. Watch who shows up in your life and see for yourself. You are not alone in building the bridge. Although it may feel as if you are out there by yourself at first, you will not be alone for long. Things will begin to make sense as to why your life seemed to "fall apart" like it did, or that relationship didn't make it, or you didn't get that job you really wanted. It is because you, on some level, chose to build the bridge, and that is certainly the road less traveled.

It's almost as if the Universe makes the decisions for you once you make the commitment, and all you have to do is practice your "why." For me, my "why" is to build the bridge, to be the bridge for others so that they may move toward a new understanding of themselves and life. And how I do that is to consciously create opportunities to empower someone, activate their soul, help them through a challenge, or simply remind them of who they are. These little acts of kindness can literally take someone from one world to another. All people really want is to be seen. When we take a moment of our time, look people square in the eye, tell them something we admire about them, and remind them of an attractive aspect of themselves, this can be life-altering and set their path of transformation into motion.

When you have stepped through to the other side of your transformation doorway, you will be welcomed with the gift of responsibility, and the ability to respond to others. It is your duty to hold the door open for those who are where you were. You can accomplish this by remaining the observer and identifying opportunities to coach, develop, inspire, motivate, mentor, teach, and influence those who seek it, those who are lost, or those just waking up from the dream. Those whose life has been "turned upside down" need some perspective as to why it is happening. You can respond and provide this perspective because you have been there. You have become the change you have always wanted to be in the world, and when others haven't noticed the spiritual binoculars hanging around their neck, you can place them in their hands. Help them see what you have seen for yourself. Create a safe space for people to grow and allow change to happen. Lift others up by sharing *your* story. Its purpose wasn't only to get you to your destiny; it happened so that you will make a difference and help someone else generate a life of purpose.

We must create sustainable change, be consistent in our

efforts to live a clean life with a clear conscience so that we may set an example for others. When you accept the path that has been laid before you, and you know beyond a shadow of a doubt this is a deep-seated passion, your spirit will be your guide and aid you by delivering your livelihood, your support system, and your resources, tools, and messages. Accept your path—begin to own and live your purpose, knowing your soul is your guide.

Self-Discovery:

- Giving is a practice. What gifts can you give that are non-monetary? (Wisdom, appreciation, a kind deed, your time, your talents, etc.)
- To whom will you give your gifts? Make a gift-giving list.
- How will you "hold the door" open for others and allow them space to grow?
- Create a Destiny Identity Affirmation:
  A. Who do you wish to help (humanity, animals, environment, worldly people, etc.)? "I help..."
  B. What do you wish to help them do or understand? "... to Do/Understand..."
  C. Why is this important and what do you wish the outcome to be from your efforts? "...so that they..."

**CHANGE
MAKERS
BOOKS**

TRANSFORMATION

Transform your life, transform your world - Changemakers
Books publishes for individuals committed to transforming their
lives and transforming the world. Our readers seek to become
positive, powerful agents of change. Changemakers Books
inform, inspire, and provide practical wisdom and skills to
empower us to write the next chapter of humanity's future.
If you have enjoyed this book, why not tell other readers by
posting a review on your preferred book site.

Recent bestsellers from Changemakers Books are:

Integration
The Power of Being Co-Active in Work and Life
Ann Betz, Karen Kimsey-House
Integration examines how we came to be polarized in our dealing
with self and other, and what we can do to move from an either/
or state to a more effective and fulfilling way of being.
Paperback: 978-1-78279-865-1 ebook: 978-1-78279-866-8

Bleating Hearts
The Hidden World of Animal Suffering
Mark Hawthorne
An investigation of how animals are exploited for
entertainment, apparel, research, military weapons, sport, art,
religion, food, and more.
Paperback: 978-1-78099-851-0 ebook: 978-1-78099-850-3

Lead Yourself First!
Indispensable Lessons in Business and in Life
Michelle Ray
Are you ready to become the leader of your own life? Apply
simple, powerful strategies to take charge of yourself, your
career, your destiny.
Paperback: 978-1-78279-703-6 ebook: 978-1-78279-702-9

Burnout to Brilliance
Strategies for Sustainable Success
Jayne Morris
Routinely running on reserves? This book helps you transform
your life from burnout to brilliance with strategies for sustainable
success.
Paperback: 978-1-78279-439-4 ebook: 978-1-78279-438-7

Goddess Calling
Inspirational Messages & Meditations of Sacred Feminine
Liberation Thealogy
Rev. Dr. Karen Tate
A book of messages and meditations using Goddess archetypes
and mythologies, aimed at educating and inspiring those with
the desire to incorporate a feminine face of God into their
spirituality.
Paperback: 978-1-78279-442-4 ebook: 978-1-78279-441-7

The Master Communicator's Handbook
Teresa Erickson, Tim Ward
Discover how to have the most communicative impact in this
guide by professional communicators with over 30 years of
experience advising leaders of global organizations.
Paperback: 978 1 78535-153-2 ebook: 978-1-78535-154-9

Meditation in the Wild
Buddhism's Origin in the Heart of Nature
Charles S. Fisher Ph.D.
A history of Raw Nature as the Buddha's first teacher, inspiring
some followers to retreat there in search of truth.
Paperback: 978-1-78099-692-9 ebook: 978-1-78099-691-2

Ripening Time
Inside Stories for Aging with Grace
Sherry Ruth Anderson
Ripening Time gives us an indispensable guidebook for growing
into the deep places of wisdom as we age.
Paperback: 978-1-78099-963-0 ebook: 978-1-78099-962-3

Striking at the Roots
A Practical Guide to Animal Activism
Mark Hawthorne
A manual for successful animal activism from an author with
first-hand experience speaking out on behalf of animals.
Paperback: 978-1-84694-091-0 ebook: 978-1-84694-653-0

Readers of ebooks can buy or view any of these bestsellers by
clicking on the live link in the title. Most titles are published
in paperback and as an ebook. Paperbacks are available in
traditional bookshops. Both print and ebook formats are available
online.

Find more titles and sign up to our readers' newsletter at
http://www.johnhuntpublishing.com/transformation
Follow us on Facebook at
https://www.facebook.com/Changemakersbooks